Island Cooking

ISLAND COOKING

Recipes from the Caribbean

DUNSTAN A. HARRIS

TEN SPEED PRESS
Berkeley/ Toronto

1⊜

Ten Speed Press
P.O. Box 7123
Berkeley, California 94707
www.tenspeed.com

Distributed in Australia by Simon and Schuster Australia, in Canada by Ten Speed Press Canada, in New Zealand by Southern Publishers Group, in South Africa by Real Books, and in the United Kingdom and Europe by Airlift Book Company.

Cover and text design by Betsy Stromberg
Illustrations on pages 8, 44, 60, 76, 80, 96, 126, and back cover by
    Raphael "Cas" Samuel

Library of Congress Cataloging-in-Publication Data

Harris, Dunstan A., 1947-
    Island cooking: recipes from the Caribbean/Dunstan A. Harris.
        p. cm.
    Includes index.
    ISBN 1-58008-501-6 (alk. paper)
    1. Cookery, Caribbean. I. Title.
TX716.A1.H37 2003
641.59729—dc21

                                                            2003045647

First printing, 2003
Printed in the United States of America

1 2 3 4 5 6 7 8 9 10 — 07 06 05 04 03

To my wife, Helen, and my two children, Jane and Alisha, who have had to endure many trial and errors but were supportive throughout the years of testing and compilation.

Contents

Acknowledgments

I am particularly indebted to the following people:

Virginia Britton, Aruba Tourist Bureau
Carol L. Crichlow, Trinidad & Tobago Tourist Board
Elyse Elkin, La Republica Dominicana
Donna Marie Freckleton, Jamaica Trade Commission
Lawrence M. Greifer, The Clement-Petrocik Co., French West Indies
Mrs. Hoyte, Guyana Consul General's Office
Kimberly Humphries, N.W. Ayer Inc., Bahamas
Gail Knopfler, Mallory Factor Inc., Netherlands Antilles Windward Islands
Rene Mack, Peter Rothholz Associates, Inc., Barbados
Susan Crea Miller, Department of Tourism, Cayman Islands
Mari V. Norris, Goya Foods
Dennis Palma, Angostura Bitters International
Catherine Randell, St. Lucia Tourist Board
Mrs. Evelyn Santiago, Puerto Rico Tourist Office
Jo-Anne Spence, word processor
Mrs. Freida Thompson, Department of Tourism, Cayman Islands.

A sincere thank-you to Andrea Chesman, my editor, who turned an idea into reality with her knack for timely coaxing and her remarkable professionalism.

Special thanks to Winston Minto, Arawak Foods, Brooklyn, New York, a friend and colleague who persuaded me to write this book.

To my wife, Helen, and my two children, Jamal and Alisha, who have had to endure many trials and errors but were supportive throughout the years of testing and compilation.

Preface

The recipes in this collection are national dishes—everyday fare and tasty bits and pieces found in Caribbean cooking. Most show the influences of the British, Dutch, French, Spanish, East Indian, West African, Portuguese, and Chinese. Because of this grand mingling of traditions, Caribbean dishes are uniquely seasoned with a little bit of this and a little bit of that. I like to describe Caribbean foods as a kind of calypso/salsa culinary medley—full of subtleties, yet pulsating.

The recipes in this collection are for those from the sunny Caribbean who have yearned for home cooking and for those who have visited the nearby tropical shores and who would like to try their hands at dishes they have enjoyed there.

It was my own nostalgia for familiar dishes that led me to try my hand at cooking. I used to write home to my mother in Jamaica to ask for recipes. Sometimes I would get so involved in a recipe, I would call her long distance to get further instructions. Eventually I mastered the fundamentals, but I was continually frustrated by the lack of many ingredients. That's when I decided to enter the business of importing Caribbean foods to the U.S. This allowed me to travel the islands extensively and to collect new recipes.

Many of the dishes in this volume have different names on different islands. To add to the confusion, ingredients in recipes from some countries are the names of recipes in others. For example, in Jamaica, callaloo is a green vegetable of the Chinese spinach family, while in Trinidad it is a dish with crab meat, pork, and callaloo leaves (dasheen or kale). It is also a soup called Pepperpot in this book.

Some of the recipes here have been donated by skilled chefs, and I thank them for their artistry. Others have been handed down from generation to generation and have withstood the passing of time.

Welcome to *Island Cooking* and bon appétit!

Introduction

In 1492, when Christopher Columbus and his forlorn crew happened upon the New World—the islands of the West Indies—his quest was to find an easier route to the spice markets of India. Columbus's navigational miscalculations opened a new chapter in world history.

Four years earlier, Bartholomeu Dias had sailed the perilous waters around Africa's Cape of Good Hope in search of spices—precious commodities at that time. Ever since Alexander the Great had invaded India in 327 B.C., Europeans had savored the pleasure of highly seasoned foods. Consequently, wars were fought, oceans braved, and continents discovered in the pursuit to dominate the spice trade. Black pepper from the peppercorn vines of the East was so valuable in Columbus's day it was traded ounce for ounce for gold.

On Columbus's second voyage to the West Indies, a physician with the party, Diego Alvarez Chanca, observed the native Arawak and Carib Indians cultivating chili peppers, which were used for cooking. Not related to the Asian peppercorn, the New World plants (of the genus *Capsicum*) were mis-named peppers because of their explosive flavor.

Although capsaicin, the substance from chili peppers, was not isolated in the laboratory until 1867, the Indians already understood that using chili peppers to season their foods not only enhanced their flavor, but also helped in their preservation—knowledge which is still employed in Caribbean house-holds that lack refrigeration. Furthermore, they found that peppers greatly aided digestion. Today, capsaicin is a major ingredient in liniments and is also used with other compounds to treat stomachaches that result from poorly functioning stomach muscles.

Garden-variety peppers, including sweet bell peppers and cayenne peppers are types of capsicum. Pickapeppa from Jamaica and Matouk's from Trinidad, similar to Tabasco from the U.S., are world-famous pepper sauces derived from capsicums.

Coincidence served as consolation for his directional blunder, and Columbus was content to return to Europe with the chili pepper as one of his important finds. Spanish and Portuguese explorers would later introduce Caribbean peppers to Africa and Asia.

In Columbus's New World, much of the Indians' diet consisted of fish—grouper, snapper, crayfish, and shrimp—which they speared from rivers and the ocean; they also ate coney (rabbit) and wild boars. Cultivated crops, such as root tubers—cassava and batata (sweet potato)—pumpkin, papaya, and pineapple are still staples in the Caribbean diet.

Pineapple did not surface in the Hawaiian islands until the nineteenth century, but Columbus came across them in 1493 on the island of Guadeloupe. Called *ananas* by the Caribs, Columbus re-christened them *la piña de las Indias* (the pine of the Indes) because they resembled "green pine cones, very sweet and delicious." Pineapples are still called *piñas* in most Spanish-speaking countries. *Mousse a l'Ananas* (Pineapple Mousse) in this collection hails from French-speaking Guadeloupe.

Papaya—paw-paw as it is called in most English-speaking islands—is another native Caribbean fruit that is now widely cultivated for commercial use throughout tropical lands. The ripe papaya is eaten as a fruit, while the green or unripe papaya is used in the preparation of condiments. The broad-veined papaya leaves are still utilized as a food tenderizer. Meats are tightly wrapped in the leaves and left over a period of time to tenderize. Today, papain, an enzyme from the fruit or leaves of papaya, is employed in the formula of many meat tenderizers.

Cassava, or yuca, is a long tuberous root that comes in two varieties—sweet and bitter. The sweet brown-skinned cassava is a permanent fixture in every open-air market in the Caribbean and grocery store found in Spanish-speaking neighborhoods in the United States. It is peeled, boiled, and treated like a vegetable. Its sibling, the bitter cassava, is an enigma! Black in skin color with rough-ridged skin, it is poisonous until cooked. The raw, grated bitter cassava is squeezed for its starchy liquid, which is used in laundering, whereas the dried grated pulp is processed into flour for use in bread and cassava cakes.

Sweet potatoes and yams are readily confused. Although both are tubers, they are from different families. Orange or purplish-brown in skin color, sweet potatoes—called *batatas* by the indigenous Indians (the word from which the English potato is derived)—were offered as a cooked mush to the earliest invaders of the Caribbean. Today it is served as a vegetable with meat dishes, or cooked in soups, or baked into pies and puddings.

A variety of winter squash, the fabled jack-o'-lantern pumpkin, is used in the U.S. for Halloween decorations and for pies. Not so in the Caribbean, where for centuries the smaller sugar pumpkin, with its smooth green and white skin, has been the basis for every self-respecting cook's Saturday Beef Soup and Pumpkin Soup.

The first land sighted and explored in the New World by Columbus was San Salvador (or Watling) Island, a part of the vast Bahamian chain. Technically in the Atlantic Ocean, the Bahamas are identified strongly with the Caribbean islands through their history and culture. This cookbook includes recipes from the Bahamas and from Cuba, of the Greater Antilles chain. Our culinary adventure moves eastward to Hispaniola (Haiti and the Dominican Republic) where, interestingly, Columbus introduced orange seeds and saplings to the New World. Recipes from Jamaica, Puerto Rico, and the smaller of the Leeward Islands—among them, the French territories of Guadeloupe and Martinique—are also included. The journey continues to islands in the Netherlands (Dutch) Antilles—Aruba, Bonaire, and Curaçao—Grenada, St. Vincent and the Grenadines (also called the Lesser Antilles), along with Barbados, which is located partially in the Caribbean Sea, with its eastern coast facing the Atlantic.

Trinidad and Tobago, the twin-island country, southernmost in the Caribbean, have the largest East Indian population of all the islands. Located on the north coast of the South American continent, Guyana, a former British colony, is the only country in South America whose inhabitants speak English. Formerly called British Guiana, it too has a significant East Indian population. Guyana is the home of the Amerindian dish Pepperpot (Meat Stew) and all kinds of tasty East Indian treats, now integral entrées in Caribbean cuisine.

Undeniably, the various waves of colonizers and immigrants to the Caribbean brought their tastes in food with them, and in time they adapted their traditional dishes to the local foods and cuisine. For example, the British Cornish pasties, a meat and potato-filled pastry, became today's Jamaican beef patty—minus the potato. Haggis, a Scottish dish of oatmeal and minced organ meats, was introduced to Barbados by the Scots after they were exiled there in 1685. Today's Barbadian Christmas treat is *jug-jug*, a casserole of millet, salted meat, green pigeon peas, and seasonings—a direct descendant of haggis. Potatoes, bacon and eggs, roast beef, pancakes, sponge cakes, rice pudding, kidney pie, Irish stew, Yorkshire pudding, smoked herring, and hot cross buns were all introduced to the Caribbean by the British.

Other European colonizers—the French, the Spanish, and to a lesser extent, the Portuguese and Dutch—passed on some of their culinary specialities to their new-found home.

French cooking methods are heavily employed in St. Martin (a half-French, half-Dutch island), Martinique, and Guadeloupe. The tiny island of Martinique, "Pearl of the Antilles," with its beautiful forested mountains and sandy beaches, boasts over one hundred first-class restaurants. Guadeloupe, a sister island and a tad larger (687 square miles), has over one hundred similarly exquisite food establishments. The islands' combination of fresh seafood and produce make them the center of haute cuisine and creole cooking (a mixture of French, African, and Eastern cuisines).

The Spanish left their imprint on three islands in particular—Cuba, Puerto Rico, and the Dominican Republic—with dishes such as Paella. And, many of the pungent variations of barbecued pork, chicken, and fish have survived since Columbus's party roasted meats on sticks over open fires and called the process *barbacoa.* Garlic pork from the Portuguese was introduced in the early seventeenth century. The Dutch islands have incorporated the mother country's famous product—cheese—into many interesting dishes, such as *Keshi Yena Coe Galinja* (Cheese with Chicken Stuffing) and a tasty snack, *Bolita de Keshi* (Cheese Balls).

The West Africans, who came to the West Indies as slaves, were eating cassava, cornmeal, yams, plantains, and bananas before their arrival. *Cou-Cou,* a dish of cornmeal with okra, popular in Barbados, is a corruption of a native West African staple, *Foo-Foo,* which is cooked and crushed cassava, yam, or plantain. *Bambula* (also a West African dance) *cake* or *bammi (bammy)* is cassava bread. Ackee, a yellow-fleshed fruit that looks and tastes like scrambled eggs, is combined with dried and salted cod fish to make an unsurpassed adventure in eating pleasure. Ackee, like many varieties of mangoes, originated in West Africa.

Jerk is a popular method of barbecuing well-seasoned pork, chicken, and fish. It has given rise to a thriving roadside fast-food industry in Jamaica. Now cooked over coals in mobile steel drum furnaces, jerked pork, a spicy-sweet and tender finger-food, can be traced to the Cormantee hunters of preslavery West Africa. During their lengthy forays over mountains and through dense vegetation, the Cormantees would roast pork over hot coals in earthen pits that were covered with *patas,* stands made of green pimento or other green tree branches. The finished jerk pork would then be cooled, stored, and reheated when needed. In Boston Beach (an area of northeastern Jamaica heavily populated by the Cormantees) today, the jerked pork is famous.

After slavery was abolished in various Caribbean territories in the nineteenth century and the newly freed slaves were unwilling to supply free labor, Chinese workers were recruited to fill the gap. Although unable to cope with the blistering heat on the region's vast banana and sugar cane plantations, the Chinese contributed their skills by opening laundries, food stores, and restaurants. Their stir-fried vegetables and sweet and sour wizardry have become a permanent part of Caribbean cuisine.

East Indians became the next source of indentured laborers, and many of today's Caribbean farms are still worked by people of East Indian ancestry. They wove their main foods—wheat flour, rice, curries, mangoes, eggplant, and ginger—into the local food tapestry.

Pelau—meat, vegetables, and rice in one dish—popular in Trinidad and throughout the Caribbean, is directly related to the many palaos, pilaffs, and pilaus of eastern India. Roti, phulouri, mango chutney, and chicken curry are just a few of the many East Indian additions to Caribbean menus.

Over the centuries, fruits and vegetables brought to the Caribbean with each wave of immigrants were planted in little plots of land given to the slaves and indentured laborers by the land owners. Through this subsistence farming, new foods were introduced to the area.

There are still vestiges of the plantation crops that were cultivated throughout the West Indies, from the sandy terrain of the Bahamas, through the volcanic recesses of the Leeward and Windward Islands, down to Guyana on the South American continent with its red-hued, fertile soil. Sugar cane (for its by-products: rum, sugar, and molasses), bananas, and pineapples are export crops that were grown on a large scale on all the islands. Although export of these cash crops has decreased, many of the original plantations— some unprofitable—still remain. Only recently have some fields been converted to raising what is needed for local consumption. Some of that acreage now boasts cattle ranches.

A lovely sight on any island is the number of urban gardens devoted to raising coconut, mango, banana, sugar cane, orange, avocado pear, pigeon peas, and peppers. In rural areas, subsistence farming provides even greater variety with backyards filled with chickens and ducks, goats, pigs, and a cow or two. Another familiar rural sight is the smokeless fireplace, a hearthstone set in concrete with a furnace at one end (in which a wood fire burns) and a flue on the other. Pots are placed on top of the heated stone. The fireplace, with its zinc roof to ward off the sun and rain, is usually located behind the main house, adjoining a raised concrete patio.

Supermarkets exist, but the traditional Caribbean open-air markets flourish under blue skies, vistas of color and movement fit for an artist's canvas. White-toothed smiles from plaid-dressed female vendors welcome strolling buyers. And everywhere are neatly stacked rows of fresh produce and fruits bearing curious names, such as coolie plum, sweetsop, soursop, naseberry, Jew plum, genip, otahiti apple, and shaddock. Sometimes the array of goods is showcased on burlap, spread on the ground, with the vendor perched atop a stool. From that vantage point, the hawk-eyed woman protects her wares from pilferage and adroitly collects and dispenses change from a deep-pocketed apron securely fastened around her waist.

Barter is still commonplace in open-air markets. Vendors are also called *higglers,* perhaps from the word *higgle* (to dispute over terms), since much haggling goes on between customers and sellers before prices are agreed on. Make no mistake about it, higglers are important to the economy of the region because they control the food supply. During a food shortage, as in Jamaica in the early 1980s, those enterprising women will board planes to neighboring countries to bring back desperately needed food items to their markets.

Fresh meats—beef, pork, mutton—and fish are sold in these traditional markets. Fish is one of the major foods on all the islands, and the best treat of all is to buy from a fisherman's catch at sunrise when tiny canoes, their nets bulging with delicacies, are pulled ashore. In Nassau, Bahamas—site of one of the richest fishing banks in the area—the brightly painted canoes are hauled ashore and nestled among the shiny pink and white conch shells that tourists buy as souvenirs. Local folk happily choose the freshly caught fish—conch, meaty grouper, multicolored snappers, and succulent lobsters—which have placed the Bahamas as a world-famous seafood paradise.

The sunrise scene of anxious buyers waiting to purchase the morning's catch is played all over the Caribbean; only the cargo varies. For example, in Barbados, Land of the Flying Fish, the gleaming silver-skinned fish of the same name is the local seafood. These small fish are boned, cleaned, and sea-soned, then steamed, or breaded and pan-fried. Sea eggs, another Barbadian favorite, is a prickly-skinned mollusk, from which the roe is extracted, then steamed or stir fried with butter and flavored with lime juice.

Although fresh fish is abundant, imported dried and salted codfish (*bacalao*) is a favorite. Codfish cakes, known by a myriad of names, are made in every corner of the Caribbean, prepared in hundreds of different ways. Called *accras* in the French islands, they are Salt Fish Fritters or Stamp and Go in Jamaica, Accra and Floats in Trinidad, and *Bacalitos* in Puerto Rico. One explanation for this widespread use of codfish, along with salted mack-erel, beef, and pork, is that salted foods needed no other method of preserva-tion and so became a ready part of the plantation diet.

Today, hamburgers, pancakes, meringue pies, and french fries are accepted in the Caribbean diet. But, by the same token, indigenous Caribbean foods have been exported to become standard fare elsewhere. And so, mixed with imported foods and the innumerable ethno-culinary blends, a potpourri has resulted that is truly Caribbean cuisine.

Raphael 'CHS' Samuel

APPETIZERS
AND SNACKS

If you have ever been to the Caribbean, you will probably remember the street markets most vividly. Close your eyes and you'll recall the smell of roast pork, eye-watering curries, and charcoal fires. Then there's the singsong of food peddlers hawking their fare on motorcycles, with makeshift coolers and ovens riding pillion, and the sight of plump bandanna-coifed females perched on little stools, arranging their slices of pepper-strewn escovitched fish, fritters, and coconut confectionary in glass cases. No doubt you sampled the hot and spicy beef patties, *chicharrones* (pork or chicken cracklings), meat-and-peas-filled rotis—all finger foods that you ate on the spot as you strolled through this unending festival.

The beef patty, similar to the Mexican emapanada and the Cornish pastie, has joined the American melting-pot, at least in New York City and its environs, as perhaps the most genuine cultural export from Jamaica. Alongside the ubiquitous pizza, the beef patty is found in pizza parlors and supermarket freezers—usually bearing the label "Tower Isle's."

In grand Caribbean fashion, most snacks are so large-portioned and filling, they often substitute for full meals. In Guadeloupe and Martinique, for example, if you aren't careful, accras (deep-fried fritters will ruin your appetite for a perfectly delicious main course.

The foods in this collection are great for in-between-meal snacks (*nix-nax* as they are called in the Caribbean), appetizers, and even side dishes. Many are superb for vegetarians. So grab your aprons and let the sun shine in.

Jamaican Beef Patties

One of Jamaica's main culinary exports, beef patties are almost as famous as rum, reggae, and Rastafarians. On my travels around the United States and Canada, I have found the Tower Isle's brand frozen beef patties in supermarket freezers. In the New York metropolitan area, and elsewhere throughout the eastern U.S., many pizza parlors carry these peppery delights. Stores that carry West Indian food products invariably have a food warmer displaying their ubiquitous snack.

Although other Caribbean islands have their versions of beef-filled pastry, Jamaica's beef patty is, by far, the tastiest.

This is my recipe, a bit all-inclusive as far as ingredients go, but well worth the effort.

1 pound lean ground beef
1 teaspoon ground annatto or
   1 tablespoon paprika for
   coloring
2 garlic cloves, crushed
1 tablespoon freshly ground
   black pepper
1 fresh hot pepper, minced
2 teaspoons seasoned salt
1 teaspoon crumbled dried
   thyme
3 large onions, finely chopped
1 cup finely chopped celery
2 tablespoons soy sauce
1/2 cup plain bread crumbs
3 scallions, finely chopped
1 tablespoon all-purpose flour
1/4 cup diced red bell pepper
Salt to taste
Patty Pastry (page 139) or
   any prepared pastry dough
1 egg yolk, slightly beaten

Combine the ground beef with the annatto or paprika in a large saucepan over medium heat, and break it up by stirring with a spoon until it is browned. Drain off any excess liquid, and add all the remaining ingredients, except the pastry and egg yolk. (If the meat is very dry, add up to 2 tablespoons water.) educe the heat, stir thoroughly, and simmer for 5 minutes. Remove from the heat and cool at room temperature.

On a floured board, roll out the pastry dough as thinly as possible—about 1/8 inch thick. Stamp out circles of dough, about 5 inches in diameter, and place 1 heaping tablespoon of the cooled beef mixture in the centre of each.

Moisten the edges of the pastry circles with water and fold the dough over to form a crescent. Crimp the edges together with a fork to seal the pastry and brush the top with the beaten egg yolk. Place on ungreased baking sheets and bake in a preheated 400°F. oven for 30 minutes. Serve warm.

To make cocktail-size patties, stamp out 2-inch or 3-inch circles of dough, fill, and bake for 20 minutes.

Yield: About 12 patties

Corn Sticks

Known as *Surullitos,* these Puerto Rican snacks are served warm with drinks, or as a side dish along with meat or fish.

1¹/2 cups water
¹/2 teaspoon salt
1 cup yellow cornmeal
1 cup freshly grated Edam,
 Gouda, or cheddar cheese
Vegetable oil for frying

Combine the water and salt in a saucepan and bring to a boil. Pour in the cornmeal slowly but steadily, and stir until the mixture is thick and smooth. Remove from the heat and stir in the cheese. Mix well and cool.

Heat about ¹/3 cup vegetable oil in a large, heavy skillet. Take small portions and shape into sticks 3 inches long and about 1 inch in diameter. Add to the hot oil and fry until golden brown all around. Drain on paper towels and cover to keep warm.

Yield: 18 corn sticks

Fried Green Plantains

Called *Banane Pesé* in the French islands, *Tostones* in the Spanish islands, this dish is found throughout the Caribbean. It is often eaten warm with meat or fish, but it is very good to eat alone. Allow 2 to 3 slices per serving. This is fun to try with kids; they especially enjoy flattening the hot pieces of plantain with their hands.

1 large green plantain, peeled
 and cut into ³/4-inch diagonal slices
Vegetable oil for frying
Salt

Soak the plantain in salted water for 30 minutes, then drain on paper towels. Heat the oil in a heavy skillet over medium high heat, add the plantain slices, and fry on both sides for about 2 minutes. Lower the heat and fry, turning constantly, for another 5 minutes.

Remove the slices from the pan and place a paper towel over them. Flatten with the palm of the hand to about half the original thickness. Return to the skillet over high heat and fry until golden brown on both sides. Drain on paper towels and salt lightly.

Yield: 4 to 6 servings

Banana Fritters

Bananas are very plentiful in the Caribbean. These fritters make a wonderful lunch treat for children. Hey also make a great snack.

3 large, very ripe bananas,
    peeled and mashed
4 tablespoons sugar
1/4 cup milk
6 tablespoons all-purpose flour
1 teaspoon baking powder
1/4 teaspoon freshly grated
    nutmeg
1 egg, beaten lightly
Vegetable oil for deep frying

Combine the bananas in a bowl with 2 tablespoons of the sugar, the milk, flour, baking powder, and nutmeg. Mix until smooth, then fold in the egg.

Heat the vegetable oil in a heavy skillet, gently add the batter by the tablespoon, and fry until golden. Sprinkle with the remaining 2 tablespoons sugar while warm. Serve warm.

Yield: 12 fritters

Phulouri

This ideal vegetarian food is found where there are large East Indian populations. Phulouri is usually dipped in a hot pepper sauce for added zest.

1 cup uncooked split peas
1 medium-size onion,
    chopped
1 garlic clove, minced
Salt an freshly ground pepper
Vegetable oil for deep frying

Soak the peas overnight in cold water to cover. Drain, combine with onion and garlic, and puree in an electric blender or food processor. Add salt and pepper to taste and beat well until fluffy.

Heat the oil in a deep-sided skillet. Shape the pea mixture into small balls, gently drop them into the hot oil, and fry until evenly brown. Drain on paper towels. Serve on toothpicks as an appetizer.

Yield: 24 split-pea balls

Eggplant Fritters ▼▲▼▲▼▲▼▲ ▼▲ ▼ ▲ ▼ ▲▼ ▲ ▼▲ ▼ ▲ ▼

Eggplant was introduced to the region by East Indian immigrants. Variations of this recipe abound in the Caribbean.

2 cups peeled and cubed eggplant
1 tablespoon white vinegar
1/2 cup water
1 egg, well beaten
1 scallion, finely chopped
1 garlic clove, minced
1 small fresh hot pepper,
   seeded and minced
1 tablespoon chopped fresh
   parsley
1/4 cup all-purpose flour
1/2 teaspoon baking powder
Salt to taste
Vegetable oil for deep frying

Combine the eggplant in a saucepan with the vinegar and water. Cover and cook over low heat until the eggplant is tender, about 20 minutes. Drain and puree in an electric blender or food processor.

Combine the pureed eggplant in a bowl with all the other ingredients, except the oil, and mix until smooth.

Heat the oil in a heavy skillet and gently drop the batter in by the tablespoon. Fry until golden brown. Drain on paper towels and serve hot as an appetizer or side dish.

Yield: 18 fritters

Conch Fritters

As the slogan goes, "It's better in the Bahamas." Nowhere else in the world is the conch prepared better than on this island chain. I have found conch, fresh and cleaned, in many New York City area and Miami fish markets. You may be able to get conch no matter where you live, so ask at your local fish market.

1 pound conch
1 small onion, finely chopped
1 celery rib, finely chopped
1/2 green pepper, seeded and
　finely chopped
1 small fresh hot pepper,
　seeded and minced
1 teaspoon dried thyme
1 tablespoon tomato paste
Salt and freshly ground
　pepper
2 cups all-purpose flour
1 teaspoon baking powder
Approximately 1 cup water
Vegetable oil for deep-frying

Pound the conch to tenderize it. Then put through a food mill or food processor to grind. Combine in a bowl with the onion, celery, green pepper, hot pepper, thyme, tomato paste, and salt and pepper to taste. Mix well. Sprinkle the flour and baking powder over the bowl and mix in until all is used. Add the water, teaspoons at a time, to make a soft batter.

Heat the oil in a large, heavy skillet. Drop the batter in by the tablespoon and fry on both sides until golden brown, using a spatula to flatten. Remove from the oil and drain on paper towels. Serve warm as a snack or an appetizer before a seafood course.

Yield: 24 fritters

Akkra ▲▽▲▽▲▽▲▽▲▽▲▽▲▽▲▽▲▽▲▽▲▽▲▽

Also spelled *Accra,* like the capital of the West African nation of Ghana, this appetizer is primarily Jamaican. Interestingly, the recipe's major ingredient, black-eyed peas or cow peas, was brought to the Americas by slave traders along with the Ashanti, fierce warriors from the Upper Volta/Ghana region of West Africa, who constituted many runaway slaves. Their descendents are still called maroons in Jamaica. In Curaçao, the fritters are called *Calas*—there they are made from the peas alone.

2 cups uncooked black-eyed peas
2 green peppers, seeded and chopped
2 fresh hot peppers, seeded and chopped
Salt to taste
Vegetable oil for frying

Soak the peas in water to cover overnight. Drain, remove and discard the skins. Cover with fresh water and soak for at least 2 hours more. Drain and combine with the peppers. Process in an electric blender or food processor until fluffy and smooth. Add salt to taste.

Heat about $1/4$ cup oil in a heavy skillet and gently drop in the mixture by the tablespoon. Fry until golden brown on both sides. Drain on paper towels. Serve warm as an appetizer.

Yield: 24 fritters

Accras de Morue

An appetizer in Martinique and Guadeloupe, breakfast fare in much of the Caribbean, these Salt Codfish Fritters make a delicious snack. Don't be surprised to see them served as a side dish as well.

1 pound salted codfish
   (bacalao), preferably
   boned
1¹/2 cups all-purpose flour
1 teaspoon baking powder
1 cup milk
1 egg
1 garlic clove, minced
1 small fresh hot pepper,
   seeded and finely chopped
¹/2 teaspoon crumbled dried
   thyme
1 teaspoon chopped fresh
   parsley (optional)
2 scallions, finely chopped
¹/2 teaspoon ground allspice
Salt and freshly ground black
   pepper
Vegetable oil for deep frying

Soak the codfish in cold water for 2 hours (or bring the water to a rolling boil and boil for 5 minutes to remove excess salt quickly). Drain, then clean the codfish of any skin and bones. Flake or finely chop and set aside.

Sift the flour and baking powder into a medium-size bowl. Whisk together the milk and egg in another bowl, then combine with the flour mixture. Add all the seasoning ingredients and flaked codfish, and mix into a sticky batter. Taste and add salt, if necessary, and pepper.

Heat the oil in a deep fryer or a large, heavy frying pan, then gently add the batter by the tablespoon and fry each side until golden brown, turning occasionally and pressing flat with a spatula. Serve hot as an appetizer, snack, or side dish.

NOTE: *The codfish can be replaced with cleaned, chopped fresh or frozen raw shrimp. Do not soak in cold water.*

Yield: 18 to 24 fritters

Codfish Balls

Here is yet another creative use of the popular dried and salted codfish. These codfish balls can be served for hors d'oeuvres on a platter with toothpicks.

1/2 pound salted codfish (bacalao), preferably boned
2 cups potatoes, peeled and diced
1 tablespoon butter
1 egg, beaten
Freshly ground pepper (optional)
Vegetable oil for deep frying

Soak the codfish in water to cover for at least 2 hours. Discard the water, then flake the fish with a fork and combine with the diced potatoes in a saucepan with fresh water. Cook until the potatoes are tender, 8 to 10 minutes; then drain.

Mash the potatoes and fish into a paste. Mix in the butter, egg, and pepper to taste. Mix well, then shape into small balls.

Heat the vegetable oil in a heavy skillet. Form the mixture into balls, about 2 teaspoons to a ball, and gently add to the oil. Fry until golden brown. Drain on paper towels and serve warm.

Yield: 18 to 24 hors d'oeuvres

Bolita di Keshi

These cheese balls from the Dutch Caribbean make a tasty appetizer. The main ingredient, Edam cheese, is usually the excess reserved from making *Keshi Yena Coe Galinja* (page 42).

1 pound Edam cheese, finely grated
6 eggs, well beaten
5 tablespoons cornstarch
Vegetable oil for deep frying

Combine the cheese, eggs, and cornstarch in a bowl and mix well. Then shape into small balls, about 2 teaspoons to a ball. Heat the vegetable oil, add the cheese balls, and fry until golden brown. Serve hot as an appetizer or party hors d'oeuvres on toothpicks.

Yield: 36 cheese balls

Stuffed Clams

Called *praires* on the French islands, clams are usually eaten raw in the Caribbean. But this recipe is unusually tasty and worth trying.

12 fresh hard-shell clams
2 cups dry white wine
2 tablespoons olive oil
3 tablespoons butter
1 teaspoon crumbled dried thyme
1 small fresh hot pepper, seeded and minced
1 medium-size onion, finely chopped
4 slices whole wheat bread, without crusts, cut into 1/4-inch cubes
Salt
1/4 cup light cream
1/4 cup grated Parmesan cheese
3 tablespoons chopped fresh parsley

Wash the clams thoroughly under cold water. In a large saucepan, bring the wine to a rolling boil. Add the clams, cover, reduce the heat, and simmer for about 5 minutes, or until the shells open. Remove the clams from the shells, chop, and set aside, reserving 12 half-shells for later use.

In a skillet, heat the olive oil and butter over medium heat. Add the thyme, hot pepper, and onion. Sauté until the onion is translucent, then add the bread cubes. Stir and sauté until the bread has soaked up all the liquid, then add the clams. Stir and taste for salt.

Remove the skillet from the heat and fill 12 half-shells with the clam mixture. Pour a little light cream over the stuffing in each shell, and sprinkle with the cheese and parsley.

Set the clams in a foil-lined baking pan and bake in a preheated 375°F oven for 5 minutes, or until lightly brown. Serve hot as an appetizer, allowing 2 clam halves per serving.

Yield: 6 servings

Stuffed Crabs ▼▲▼▲▼▲▼▲▼▲▼▲▼▲▼▲▼▲▼▲▼▲

From the French Caribbean, the secret to this splendid recipe is in the addition of the rum and hot pepper.

6 to 8 live blue crabs (or
   1¹/₂ pounds crab meat)
1¹/₂ cups fresh unseasoned
   bread crumbs
1 large fresh hot pepper,
   seeded and minced
3 tablespoons dark rum
2 garlic cloves, crushed
¹/₄ teaspoon ground allspice
2 tablespoons chopped fresh
   parsley
1 tablespoon lime or lemon
   juice
Salt
2 tablespoons butter, at room
   temperature

Cook the live crabs in a large pot of boiling water for 10 minutes. Let them cool, then remove the meat from the shells and claws, and mince. Scrub the shells thoroughly and lay them aside.

Combine the crab meat and 1 cup of the bread crumbs in a bowl and mash into a paste. Add the hot pepper, rum, garlic, allspice, parsley, lime or lemon juice, and salt to taste. Mix well. Stuff the crab shells (or scallop shells if fresh, frozen, or canned crab meat is used) with the mixture, sprinkle over the remaining ¹/₂ cup bread crumbs, and dot with the softened butter. Bake in a preheated 350°F oven for 30 minutes. Serve hot as an appetizer, side dish, or lunch.

Yield: 6 to 8 servings

Féroce d'Avocat ▲▽▲▽▲▽▲▽▲▽▲▽▲▽▲▽▲▽

Another French Caribbean entry, this Peppery Avocado Puree, a distant cousin of guacamole, is found in several variations throughout other islands. The cassava meal is used to add body, but I have found fine, unseasoned bread crumbs make an excellent substitute.

1/4 pound salted codfish
(bacalao), preferably boned
1 medium-size ripe avocado,
peeled and diced
1/2 cup vegetable oil
1/4 cup lime or lemon juice
1 garlic clove, crushed
2 fresh hot peppers, seeded
and chopped
1 tablespoon chopped fresh
parsley
Pinch sugar
1/2 cup cassava meal (manioc
meal) or fine unseasoned
dried bread crumbs
1/4 cup coconut milk
(page 149)
Salt and freshly ground pepper

Soak the codfish in cold water to cover for 3 to 4 hours. Drain, then rinse under cold water. Pat dry. Place under a broiler and broil until brown, turning to cook on both sides. Cool, then shred finely with a fork.

In a bowl, mash the avocado, and stir in the shredded codfish. In another bowl, mix a dressing of oil, lime or lemon juice, garlic, hot peppers, parsley, and sugar. Pour the dressing over the avocado paste, add the cassava meal or bread crumbs and coconut milk, then mix to form a thick paste. Taste and add salt and pepper, if desired. Serve on crackers as a canapé.

Yield: 2 1/2 cups

Solomon Gundy

The name and the dish are obvious corruptions of *salmigondis,* a seventeenth-century French salad plate of chopped meat, anchovies, eggs, and vegetables. This recipe is primarily Jamaican. The U.S. Virgin Islands' herring gundy is similar, but more elaborately prepared. A party favorite, this dish is also available bottled commercially. The pickled fish ingredients are available in West Indian food stores and Spanish *bodegas.*

2 pounds pickled herring
1/2 pound pickled mackerel
1/2 pound pickled shad
1 cup white vinegar
1 tablespoon allspice berries
3 scallions, finely chopped
2 fresh hot peppers, seeded
   and minced
1 large onion, finely chopped
1/4 cup vegetable oil
Freshly ground pepper

Soak the fish in cold water to cover for at least 2 hours. Drain, then place in a saucepan with fresh water to cover, and bring to a quick boil. Drain again, then remove the fish from the saucepan and cool. Clean and discard all skin and bones, then shred the meat finely through a food mill or in a food processor.

Combine the vinegar and allspice berries in another saucepan and bring to a rolling boil.

Place the fish in a deep dish and mix in the scallions, hot peppers, and onion. Pour over the vegetable oil, the vinegar and allspice, and freshly ground black pepper to taste. Stand covered at room temperature overnight. Remove and discard the allspice. Store the gundy in a covered jar and refrigerate for further use.

Serve as a spread on crackers for a canapé.

Yield: 3 cups

Escovitched Fish ▲▼▲▼▲▼▲▼▲▼▲▼▲▼▲▼▲▼▲▼

A snack, full meal, or a finger food, Pickled Fish is found in all corners of the Caribbean, especially in the ubiquitous glass cases in bars and restaurants. This recipe is primarily Jamaican, but parallels one from the Spanish islands, *Pescado en Escabeche*. The Spanish choice of fish is swordfish, haddock, or shad. Sometimes the fish is marinated for up to a week with a cup of green olives. This pickling process is very old and goes back to pre-refrigeration times. The fish will keep for days without spoiling.

3 pounds fish (snapper or any large fish), cut in 1/2-inch slices
2 limes or lemons, sliced
1 tablespoon salt
1 tablespoon freshly ground black pepper
1/4 cup all-purpose flour
1 cup vegetable oil (olive oil is recommended for the Spanish version; coconut oil is used on the other islands)
1 bay leaf
1/2 cup malt vinegar
1 teaspoon whole allspice berries
2 large onions, sliced
1 fresh hot pepper, sliced

Wash the fish thoroughly in cold water and rub lime or lemon over the slices. Rinse and pat dry with paper towels, then season the fish with the salt and pepper and allow to stand for 30 minutes.

Dust the slices of fish with a thin coating of flour.

Heat the oil in a large skillet and fry the fish or both sides until crisp and brown. Let the fish cool in a dish. Combine the bay leaf, vinegar, allspice, onions, and hot pepper in a saucepan and cook until the onions are tender. Cool, then pour the mixture over the fish and cover. Marinate for at least 2 hours at room temperature or overnight in the refrigerator. Serve cold or at room temperature. Spoon the marinade and spices over the fish as you serve.

To make this into a complete meal, serve with a vegetable salad and French bread.

Yield: 6 servings

SOUPS

In the old days, agricultural workers—slaves and indentured servants—began their long shifts on the sugar cane and banana plantations in the pre-dawn darkness. It was their custom to pool together each day a variety of vegetables raised from their individual subsistence garden plots, any scraps of meat that were available, as well as their rations of flour and salted meats. At that very early hour, the designated cook would create a soup in a huge wrought-iron cauldron placed over a coal fire to slowly cook for several hours. At mid-day, when the workers broke for lunch, soup, perhaps the day's most complete and nutritious meal, was served. Even today in the fields, or at any work site where large numbers of workers gather outdoors, this practice continues.

From these humble beginnings, many soup recipes have become vital parts of the Caribbean's cuisine. Soups with a fish or seafood base are likely to have originated in those islands with rich fishing banks, such as the Bahamas. Soups rich in meats and vegetables are popular on islands such as Jamaica, which has strong agricultural traditions.

The soups offered to visitors to the Caribbean are almost always strained and the broth served as an appetizer (with the meat and vegetables saved to be reheated later for a family dinner). But in a familiar setting, or with a family, soup is usually a main course, rich in meat and vegetables. I remember in my house that Saturday's noon meal was a steaming bowl of beef soup—ninety degree weather and all. It was a great disappointment if guests were dining, for then my mother followed the custom of straining the soup to impress them.

To my delight, today most households—in Jamaica and other Caribbean countries—still serve a hearty soup for that Saturday meal.

Although the soup recipes collected here are indeed traditional fare from the Caribbean, some recipes may seem strikingly familiar. Chick-Pea Soup is remarkably similar to split-pea soup; and the Fisherman's Soup has a kinship with a good Manhattan clam chowder.

Hard-to-find ingredients can be replaced with similar foods; for example, ham hocks can replace pig's tail, and root vegetables such as dasheen can be replaced with potato. But truly, from Boston to Los Angeles, Detroit, and Miami, every large city has Spanish *bodegas* or Caribbean food stores where most of the soup ingredients can be found. Some meat and fish items not readily found in the local supermarket can be special ordered from a butcher or fishmonger.

Conch Chowder

The conch, a mollusk, is renowned for its beautiful shell. Put to the ear, the listener hears the sound of the sea. The shell is also used as a horn. Oftimes the delicious meat is ignored, even though it is used extensively in the Bahamas and the French Caribbean islands in salads, fritters, and stews. The old Carib name for the conch is *lambie* or *lambi,* which is still used in the French Caribbean and some eastern Caribbean islands. To the Spanish, it is *concha.* The conch is usually pounded to tenderize it; as a result, a saying in Creole by wife beaters goes: *"I bat li con lambi,"* which translates, "I beat her like a conch."

This chowder, sometimes called Conch Soup in many islands, is a good appetizer for a seafood entree.

1 pound fresh conch meat, pounded
Lime or lemon juice
2 quarts water
2 celery ribs, chopped
1 christophene (chayote), peeled and diced
4 carrots, diced
4 small potatoes, peeled and diced
1 medium-size onion, diced
1 garlic clove, crushed
1 sprig fresh thyme
1 teaspoon Hot Pepper Sauce (page 92) or Tabasco sauce
Salt and freshly ground pepper

Thoroughly wash the conch in lime or lemon juice, then cut into small pieces. Combine with the water in a medium-size saucepan and cook over low heat for 2 hours. Add the celery, christophene, carrots, potatoes, onion, garlic, and thyme, and simmer for 30 minutes. About 15 minutes before removing from the heat, add the pepper sauce, and salt and freshly ground pepper to taste. Serve hot.

Yield: 4 to 6 appetizer servings

Fish Chowder

This is also called Fish Tea and Fish Soup on some islands. The straining process is often skipped if a bony fish is not used. Flour dumplings (page 142) can be added if this is to be served as a meal instead of an appetizer. As the dumplings cook, the soup will be slightly thickened, making the name chowder much more appropriate. A quartered medium-sized tomato, a peeled and sliced christophene (chayote), and a diced carrot can be added, if desired, after the first 30 minutes of cooking.

2 pounds fresh fish, any variety
2 quarts water
6 allspice berries
1 sprig fresh thyme
1 fresh whole hot pepper
4 small potatoes, peeled
4 whole green bananas, peeled
Salt

Clean and thoroughly wash the fish. Combine with the water in a large heavy saucepan, cover, and cook over medium heat for 30 minutes. Remove the fish, reserving the stock in the saucepan, then remove and discard all fish bones. Return the fish to the saucepan and add the allspice, thyme, hot pepper, potatoes, bananas, and salt to taste. Stir and simmer, removing the whole pepper after 10 minutes. Continue to simmer for 30 minutes. Taste for salt, remove the allspice and thyme sprig, and serve hot.

Yield: 4 appetizer servings

Fisherman's Soup

Expensive to make, this soup is from the Netherlands Antilles where seafood is much more affordable. It is sometimes garnished with croutons or toast rounds and a tablespoon of mayonnaise.

1 medium-size lobster, cooked, or 1/2 pound cooked lobster meat
1/4 pound raw shrimp with shells
1/2 pound white-fleshed fish fillet
6 cups chicken stock
1 onion, sliced
2 potatoes, peeled and sliced
2 bay leaves, crumbled
2 garlic cloves
2 tablespoons tomato paste
2 large tomatoes, seeded and chopped
1/4 cup cooking sherry
Salt and freshly ground pepper
1 tablespoon butter

If the lobster and shrimp are in their shells, remove and chop the meat, reserving the shells.

Combine the fish fillet with the chicken stock in a large saucepan and poach until the fish flakes easily. Remove the fish from the stock, chop, and set aside with the lobster and shrimp. Add the reserved shells (if used) to the stock and cook over medium heat for 15 minutes, then remove and discard the shells. Add all the ingredients, except the seafood and butter, to the stock and cook for another 15 minutes. Remove the saucepan from the heat and blend the soup in batches in an electric blender or food processor. Return the blended stock to heat, stir in the butter, and add the seafood. Cover and simmer for 5 minutes. Serve hot.

Yield: 6 appetizer servings

Callaloo Soup

Callaloo Soup is also known as Pepperpot Soup, but should not to be confused with the dish Callaloo from the eastern Caribbean or the Guyanese Pepperpot. This is perhaps the most famous of all Caribbean soups. Versions are as varied as its spelling: *Calaloo, Callilu, Calalou,* and *Callau.* The name is derived from the leaves of certain plants with edible tubers: among them dasheen, eddoe, taro, and tannia. A broad-leafed spinach, the Caribbean callaloo plant is also used in this soup. It is Chinese spinach or yin choi, Japanese hiyu, East Indian bhagi, and is closely related to the Swiss chard.

This recipe is mine, created by borrowing here and dropping ingredients there.

1/2 pound salted or fresh pig's tail, chopped (or 2 small smoked ham hocks)

1 pound salted beef or stewing beef, cubed

4 quarts cold water

1 1/2 pounds fresh callaloo or spinach, chopped, or 2 (10-ounce) packets frozen spinach

12 fresh okras or 1 (10-ounce) frozen packet

1/2 cup coconut milk (page 149) (optional)

3 medium-size potatoes, peeled and sliced in half

1 whole fresh hot pepper

1 medium-size onion, chopped

1 garlic clove, minced

1 scallion, chopped

1 sprig fresh thyme

Salt

Soak the salted meats in water to cover for at least 2 hours, preferably overnight. Drain. Then combine all the salted meats with fresh water to cover in a heavy saucepan and bring to a rolling boil. Drain and discard the water. Repeat if the meats are still salty.

Add the 4 quarts of cold water to the saucepan. Then add the stewing beef (if used) callaloo or spinach, and okra. Return to the heat and bring to a quick boil. Lower the heat and simmer for an hour or until the meat is tender. Stir in the coconut milk. After 15 minutes, add the potatoes, hot pepper, onion, garlic, scallion, and thyme. Stir, taste for flavor, and add salt if required. Allow the soup to simmer over medium heat for another 45 minutes, or until thickened. Remove the whole pepper and thyme sprig before serving.

NOTE: *Chopped kale or dasheen leaves can be substituted for the callaloo or a part of the spinach. Chicken stock can be a substitute for a part of the water. Flour dumplings and any assortment of root vegetables can be added 30 minutes before the soup has finished cooking. The soup can be strained or pureed in small portions and served without any meat or vegetables as an appetizer for 8 to 10 people.*

Yield: 6 main course servings

Le Pâte en Pot ▲▽▲▽▲▽▲▽▲▽▲▽▲▽▲▽▲▽▲▽

A traditional dish from Martinique, this heavy soup is usually served at engagement parties, weddings, christenings, and similar festive occasions. Often a whole lamb is roasted for the occasion, and the fresh entrails are used as ingredients for this recipe.

A similar dish is served at the same festive occasions in Jamaica and is called Mannish Water (mannish closely parallels macho). There the lamb entrails are replaced with a goat's, and the cabbage, dry wine, capers, and cognac are replaced with a liberal quantity of Jamaican white rum (181% proof), a fiery hot fresh pepper, and, perhaps, a few peeled green bananas added 30 minutes before the soup is done.

4 quarts water (or enough to
   cover the lamb)
2 pounds lamb entrails, head,
   and feet, cleaned, or
   2 pounds lamb or goat
   stew meat
2 small onions, chopped
1 celery rib, chopped
2 garlic cloves, minced
4 whole cloves
2 bay leaves
Salt and freshly ground pepper
1/2 cup vegetable oil
4 medium-size carrots, diced
3 turnips, peeled and cubed
4 medium-size potatoes,
   peeled and cubed
1/4 pound raw pumpkin,
   peeled and cubed
3 scallions, chopped
1 pound cabbage, chopped
2 cups dry white wine
1 tablespoon cognac
1/2 cup capers

In a large, heavy saucepan, combine the water, meat, onions, celery, garlic, cloves, bay leaves, and salt and pepper to taste. Bring to a rolling boil, skimming off any fats. Cover and continue to cook over medium heat for 30 minutes. Remove the meat and cut into small pieces, discarding the bones. Then strain and reserve the stock.

In another saucepan, heat the oil over medium heat. Add the meat, carrots, turnips, potatoes, pumpkin, scallions, and cabbage. Sauté for 5 minutes, then combine with the reserved stock and simmer for 2 hours. Add the wine, cognac, and capers. Stir and taste for salt and pepper. Continue to simmer for about 10 minutes. Serve hot.

Yield: 10 to 12 appetizer servings

Beef Soup

My own variation of a Jamaican Saturday Soup, this is generally served around noontime as the day's deliciously filling meal.

The pumpkin should be very ripe for easy dissolving. In Jamaica, about 30 minutes before the soup is finished, I would add a whole Scotch bonnet, the flavorful island pepper, and remove it before serving. Dumplings, fresh corn, peeled potatoes, and any number of root vegetables can be added after the first 2 hours of cooking.

1¹/2 pounds soup bones or
   stewing beef, cubed
3 to 4 quarts water
3 carrots, sliced
1 christophene (chayote),
   peeled and diced
1 turnip, peeled and diced
1 pound pumpkin, peeled
   and cubed
Salt
1 teaspoon freshly ground
   black pepper
2 scallions, chopped
1 ounce vermicelli

Combine the soup bones or stewing beef with the water (use 4 quarts for a thinner soup) in a covered saucepan and cook over medium heat for 1 hour. Add the carrots, christophene, turnip, and pumpkin. Cook over medium heat for 30 minutes. Add salt to taste, the pepper, scallions, and vermicelli and simmer for another hour. Serve hot.

Yield: 6 main course servings

Pigeon Pea Soup

Called *gungo peas* in Jamaica and Trinidad and *gandules* or *gandures* in Spanish-speaking areas, the peas are ubiquitous in the Caribbean, growing wild in many backyards.
The Spanish, in their dish *Sopa de Gandules,* often add 2 teaspoons of lard colored with annatto or saffron, sweet peppers, a cup of rice, or a pound of pumpkin about 30 minutes before the end of the cooking time.

*1/2 pound salted pig's tail or
   2 small smoked ham hocks*
1/4 pound salted beef
1 pound stewing beef
*4 quarts water or chicken
   stock*
*2 cups uncooked green or
   dried pigeon peas or
   2 (16-ounce) cans,
   drained*
1 onion, chopped
1 scallions, chopped
1 sprig dried thyme
4 potatoes, peeled and sliced
Salt

Soak the salted meat in water to cover for at least 2 hours, preferably overnight. Drain. Add fresh water, bring to a boil, then drain again. Combine all the meats with 4 quarts of fresh water or chicken stock, cover, and bring to a boil. Add the green or dried peas (not canned), reduce the heat, and cook, covered, for 1 hour. Add the canned peas (if used) and the onion, scallion, thyme, and potatoes. Add salt to taste. If you like, add any other vegetables (carrots or yams) or dumplings. Simmer for 1 hour. Serve hot.

Yield: 6 to 8 main course servings

Red Pea Soup

The red peas, as they are called on some islands, are the California pink beans or the Mexican chili beans. The red kidney bean makes a good stand-in. This dish is found throughout the Caribbean. In the U.S. Virgin Islands, where it is called Red Bean Soup, a pinch of sugar, chopped celery, and sliced ripe plantain are added.

1 pound salted pig's tail, chopped, or 1 pound smoked ham hocks
1 pound stewing beef, cubed
2 cups dried kidney beans or 1 (16-ounce) can
4 quarts water
3 to 4 small potatoes, peeled and cubed
1/2 cup coconut milk (page 149) (optional)
1 onion, chopped
2 scallions, chopped
1 sprig fresh thyme
1 whole fresh hot pepper
Salt

Soak the pig's tail overnight in fresh water to cover. Then thoroughly rinse the pig's tail or ham hocks in cold water. Combine in a large, heavy saucepan with the beef, dried kidney beans (do not add canned beans at this time), and the water. Cover and cook over medium heat for about 1 hour, until the meat and beans are tender. Add the potatoes, coconut milk, and any other peeled root vegetables or dumplings along with the onion, scallions, thyme, and hot pepper. (If canned beans are used, add at this time.) Add salt to taste. Stir the soup and allow to simmer for 1 hour. Remove the whole hot pepper and thyme sprig before serving. Serve hot. This soup is even better served the second day.

Yield: 6 to 8 main course servings

Chick-Pea Soup

Chick-peas are called *garbanzos* by the Spanish, and when pureed with spices and other ingredients, they comprise the well-known Middle Eastern falafel. The Spanish version of this recipe requires that the meat and tomato paste be sautéed in a tablespoon of olive oil before they are added to the water.

1 pound stewing beef
8 cups water
Salt
1 (11-ounce) can cooked
   chick-peas, drained
2 medium-size potatoes,
   peeled and diced
2 ounces vermicelli
1/2 teaspoon garlic powder
1/2 teaspoon onion powder
1/4 teaspoon ground cumin
2 tablespoons tomato paste

In a large saucepan, combine the stewing beef, water, and salt to taste. Bring to a boil, reduce the heat, and cook over medium heat for 1 hour. Add the chick-peas, potatoes, and vermicelli and continue to cook over medium heat for 30 minutes. Stir in the garlic powder, onion powder, cumin, and tomato paste and cook for another 20 minutes, until the soup has thickened. Serve hot.

Yield: 4 to 6 main course servings

Peanut Soup

This soup is found in the Dutch Caribbean and in English-speaking St. Kitts, where peanuts are called groundnuts. One cup of heavy cream can replace the milk if a heavier consistency and richer taste is preferred. A jigger of dry sherry is also encouraged. This soup is sometimes served chilled and garnished with chopped chives.

1 1/2 cups dry unsalted roasted
   peanuts
3 cups chicken stock
1 large onion, finely chopped
1 teaspoon hot pepper sauce
Salt
1 tablespoon soy sauce
1 1/2 cups milk, scalded
Croutons

In a blender or food processor, combine the peanuts and some chicken stock and puree. In a saucepan, combine the pureed peanuts, the remainder of the chicken stock, the onion, hot pepper sauce, and salt to taste. Cook over low heat for 15 minutes, stirring occasionally. Stir in the soy sauce and milk, and continue cooking over low heat for another 5 minutes. Garnish with croutons and serve hot.

Yield: 6 appetizer servings

Gouda Cheese Soup

Here is another entry from the Dutch islands. It is remarkably similar to some French onion soup recipes, but the garlic replaces the onions.

4 medium-size carrots, diced
5 cups chicken stock
1/4 pound butter
2 teaspoons all-purpose flour
2 garlic cloves, crushed
2 cups freshly grated Gouda
   cheese
Salt and freshly ground pepper

Combine the carrots and chicken stock in a saucepan over medium heat and cook for 15 minutes.

In a skillet, melt the butter and add the flour, stirring until a thick paste is formed. Add the garlic and cheese and continue to stir over medium heat until smooth. Stir the cheese mixture into the chicken stock, and continue cooking over medium heat for another 5 minutes. Add salt and pepper to taste and serve hot.

Yield: 4 appetizer servings

Pumpkin Soup

This Caribbean favorite is found mainly in hotel restaurants.

1/2 pound salted beef, cubed,
   or 1/2 pound salted pig's
   tail, chopped
1 pound stewing beef, cubed
2 quarts water
2 pounds pumpkin, peeled
   and diced
2 scallions, chopped
1 garlic clove, crushed
1 sprig fresh thyme
1 whole fresh hot pepper
Salt

Soak the salted meat in water to cover for at least 2 hours, preferably overnight. Discard the water. Combine the meats with 2 quarts of fresh water in a covered saucepan, and cook over medium heat for 1 hour. Add the diced pumpkin and cook for another hour, or until the pumpkin is dissolved. Add the scallions, garlic, thyme, pepper, and more water, if needed. Add salt to taste, stir, and simmer for 30 minutes. Remove the thyme sprig and whole hot pepper before serving. Serve hot.

NOTE: *Chicken stock can replace the water and a cup of heavy cream can be added. Also, if the pumpkin is not completely dissolved, the finished soup can be passed through a sieve for a smoother consistency.*

Yield: 4 appetizer servings

Avocado Cream Soup

Served in some Caribbean hotels at poolside, this is a tasty cold soup for those hot, tropical days. Avocados are simply called pears on the islands.

2 large ripe avocados, peeled and chopped
3/4 cup half and half
2 cups chicken stock
1/2 teaspoon hot pepper sauce
Salt and freshly ground pepper

Place the chopped avocados in an electric blender or food processor and puree. Add the half and half and blend well.

Combine the chicken stock with the avocado puree in a bowl, stirring well. Pass the mixture through a sieve, then stir in the hot pepper sauce, and add salt and black pepper to taste. Refrigerate for at least 2 hours before serving.

Yield: 2 appetizer servings

CHICKEN, FISH, AND MEATS

Jerked chicken, fish, and pork is beginning to claim a position as the most popular of Caribbean dishes to influence North American menus. Jerk is a centuries-old method of roasting meat in earthen pits that dates back centuries in Jamaica. It was probably developed by the Cormantees, the West Africans who became the island's runaway slaves (maroons) of the seventeenth century. It is my guess that the Arawak Indians' method of preparing pork for barbecuing—especially using the chili pepper for seasoning—was combined with the Cormantees' pit cooking to give rise to today's pungent barbecue.

When I was growing up in Jamaica, pork was the only meat jerked, and the traditional cooking was confined to the Portland area in the northeastern reaches of the island, haven to the runaway slaves. Today jerk joints are found across the island, and they serve chicken and fish as well as pork.

If you are looking for a quintessential Caribbean dish to begin your culinary experiments with, you can't go wrong with the spicy sweet flavor of jerk.

Basic Jerk Seasoning

The single factor that makes it possible to simulate the taste of jerk is the seasoning. Cooks, housewives, and entrepreneurs have begun to whip up their own variations of jerk seasoning—and the earthen pit is no longer required. Jerk can be made on a grill or in the oven with excellent results.

2 ounces Jamaican pimento
    (allspice), crushed
1/4 teaspoon freshly grated
    nutmeg
1 teaspoon ground cinnamon
12 scallions, cleaned and
    chopped
6 Scotch Bonnet or
    12 jalapeño peppers,
    halved with seeds
1/2 cup red wine vinegar
2 tablespoons vegetable oil
1 tablespoon salt
1 teaspoon freshly ground
    black pepper
2 tablespoons soy sauce
Hot pepper sauce (optional)

Combine all the ingredients in a blender or food processor, adding hot pepper sauce to taste. Process to liquefy for 1 minute. Pour into a jar and refrigerate until you are ready to use it.

Yield: Approximately 1 cup

Jerked Chicken, Pork, and Fish

This recipe is for a barbecue party of 6 to 8 people. You can use any combination of meats and fish. If pimento wood chips are available, add them to the coals for genuine jerk flavor or soak whole pimento berries in water and add them to the fire.

6 to 8 loin pork chops cut
    1-inch thick
6 chicken thighs
6 chicken drumsticks
6 to 8 fish steaks or fillets
Lime or lemon juice
1 recipe Basic Jerk Seasoning

Wash the pork, chicken, and/or fish separately in lime or lemon juice. Rinse under cold water and pat dry.

Place the meat in a deep, non-aluminum baking dish and pour half of the jerk seasoning over. Rub the seasoning evenly over all. In another baking dish, use 1 tablespoon of the seasoning mix for each pound of fish and rub in carefully. Cover and refrigerate at least 3 hours or overnight.

If you want to eat the fish first, followed by the chicken and later the pork, by all means put everything on the grill at once. The fish will be done first, the chicken second, and the pork last. However, if you prefer to have everything served together, start to cook the pork first, the chicken next, and the fish last.

Slowly cook over hot coals or on a gas-heated barbecue at least 6 inches from the heat source on a very low setting. Cover with aluminum foil or the barbecue lid, leaving the vents slightly open. Allow about 2 hours for the pork, 1 1/2 hour for the chicken, and 20 minutes for the fish, depending on thickness of the fish steak or fillet. Check the fish to see if it flakes easily before removing. Check the chicken and pork for doneness before removing. Baste everything frequently; the chicken and pork can be turned occasionally.

Remove the meats from the grill and allow to stand for about 10 minutes for the meat to reabsorb the juices.

Yield: 6 to 8 servings

Arroz con Pollo

1/4 cup vegetable oil
3-pound chicken, cut into
    portion-sized pieces
1 onion, chopped
1 garlic clove, minced
1 green pepper, chopped
1 cup stewed tomatoes
1/2 teaspoon salt
1/4 teaspoon freshly ground
    black pepper
1 bay leaf
1/2 teaspoon paprika
1 cup dry white wine
2 cups uncooked rice
1 (10-ounce) package
    green peas, thawed, or
    1 (12-ounce) can, drained

Heat the oil in a large skillet, add the chicken pieces a few at a time, and sauté evenly to a golden brown. Add the onion, garlic, and green pepper and sauté until the onion is translucent. Add the tomatoes, salt, black pepper, bay leaf, and paprika. Bring to a boil, cover, and simmer for 30 minutes. Add the wine and rice, stir well, cover, and simmer for about 20 minutes, or until the rice is tender. Sprinkle the peas over the top and cook, uncovered, for 5 more minutes. Serve hot for lunch or dinner.

Yield: 6 servings

Asopao de Pollo

2 cups rice
Salt and freshly ground
    pepper
3-pound chicken, cut into
    portion-sized pieces
3 tablespoons lard or
    vegetable oil
Sofrito (page 137)
1 cup tomato sauce
6 cups chicken stock or water
1 cup cooked green peas
Pimientos
Cooked asparagus tips

Soak the rice in water to cover for about 30 minutes. Rub salt and pepper into the chicken pieces. Heat the lard or vegetable oil in a large, heavy saucepan, add the chicken pieces a few at a time, and sauté until lightly golden. Stir in the sofrito and the tomato sauce. Reduce the heat, cover, and cook for 15 minutes.

Drain the rice and add to the saucepan. Cover and cook for 5 minutes. Add the chicken stock or water and taste for salt and pepper. Cover and cook over low heat for about 20 minutes, or until rice is tender but very moist. Garnish with green peas, pimientos, and asparagus tips. Serve hot.

Yield: 6 servings

Chicken in Coconut Milk

This dish is claimed by the French island of Martinique under the name of *Fricassée de Poulet au Coco*. But the method of cooking chicken in coconut milk, which gives the chicken a sweet flavor, shows up elsewhere with slight variations. In Haiti, you'll find *Poulet à la Creole* (Chicken Creole Style), which is spiced with a few teaspoons of curry powder and a hint of powdered saffron.

3-pound chicken fryer, cut into portion-sized pieces
1/4 cup coconut oil (page 150)
1 onion, finely chopped
1 garlic clove, minced
1/4 pound mushrooms, sliced
2 cups coconut milk (page 149)
Salt and pepper
1 sprig fresh parsley
1 small fresh hot pepper
1 teaspoon dried thyme or 1 sprig fresh

Towel dry the chicken. In a large, heavy skillet, heat the oil. Add the chicken pieces and fry until lightly browned. Remove from the skillet and set aside. In the same skillet, sauté the onion, garlic, and mushrooms for about 3 minutes. Return the chicken to the skillet and add the coconut milk and salt and pepper to taste. Tie the parsley, hot pepper, and thyme in a cheesecloth pouch to form a bouquet garni, and add to the skillet. Cover and simmer until the chicken is tender, about 1 1/4 hours. Remove the bouquet garni and serve the chicken with rice.

Yield: 6 servings

Keshi Yena Coe Galinja ▲▽▲▽▲▽▲▽▲▽▲▽▲▽▲

You will also see Cheese with Chicken Stuffing spelled as *Keshy Yena,* meaning stuffed or filled cheese in the patois of the Dutch Caribbean. This is also the Spanish *Queso Relleno.* A tasty entrée, it is much simpler to prepare than appears.

3-pound to 4-pound Edam cheese
2 pounds chicken, preferably breasts and thighs
1 onion, finely chopped
Salt and pepper
1 teaspoon poultry seasoning
2 tablespoons butter
2 onions, sliced
3 tomatoes, peeled, seeded, and chopped
1 large green pepper, seeded and chopped
1 tablespoon fresh parsley leaves
hot pepper sauce to taste
2 tablespoons tomato paste
1/4 cup sliced pimiento-stuffed olives
1 tablespoon capers
1/4 cup raisins
2 tablespoons chopped gherkins

Strip the outer wax wrapping from the cheese and cut off about an inch from the top. Scoop out the cheese leaving a shell about 1 inch thick. Put the shell aside, and use the scooped-out cheese in another recipe, such as *Bolita di Keshi* (page 17) or Corn Sticks (page 11).

Rub the chicken pieces with the chopped onion, salt and pepper to taste, and poultry seasoning. Let stand for at least 2 hours at room temperature.

Arrange the chicken in a baking dish and broil until brown. Remove from the broiler and bake at 350°F for 1 hour. Remove any skin and bones and shred the meat into fine pieces.

Heat the butter in a large skillet and add the sliced onions, tomatoes, green pepper, parsley, and hot pepper sauce. Sauté for about 3 minutes, stirring regularly. Stir in the tomato paste, olives, capers, raisins, gherkins, and shredded chicken. Reduce the heat and simmer for about 20 minutes. Remove from the heat and cool.

Stuff the reserved cheese shell with the chicken mixture and top with the cheese lid. Place the filled shell in a large greased casserole. Bake in a preheated 350°F oven for about 30 minutes, or until the cheese becomes soft. Transfer to a serving dish and cut into wedges to serve.

Yield: 6 to 8 servings

Chicharrones de Pollo

Pass any Spanish restaurant in the United States and you will surely see *chicharrones,* not only on the menu, but prominent on a sign in the window. Roughly translated, *chicharrones* means pork cracklings, which is also a popular finger-food. Somehow the translation encompasses the way chicken is done is this recipe.

Chicharrones de Pollo is the Kentucky Fried Chicken of the Spanish Caribbean, meaning it is just as popular, but a lot more flavorful. Street vendors push gaily painted carts and hawk this dish, which is eaten as a snack or a meal.

2 pounds boneless chicken,
preferably breast meat,
cut into 2-inch slices
Lime or lemon juice
2 tablespoons brandy or rum
1/2 teaspoon seasoned salt
1 tablespoon malt vinegar
Salt
1 cup all-purpose flour
1 teaspoon baking powder
2 cups vegetable oil

Wash the chicken well with lime or lemon juice. Combine the brandy or rum, seasoned salt, vinegar, and salt to taste in a dish. Add the chicken and marinate for at least 2 hours at room temperature.

Combine the flour and baking powder, and more salt, if desired, in a plastic bag. Remove the chicken from the marinade and place in the plastic bag with the flour. Shake to coat each piece evenly.

Heat the vegetable oil in a large, heavy skillet, add the chicken, and fry evenly until tender and golden brown, about 5 minutes for each side. Briefly drain the chicken and serve hot.

Yield: 4 servings

Raphael 'CRS' Samuel

Fricasséed Duck

4-pound duckling
¹/4 cup lime or lemon juice
Salt
1 onion, chopped
1 sprig fresh thyme
1 scallion, chopped
1 hot pepper, seeded and
    sliced
1 tablespoon white vinegar
1 garlic clove, minced
2 medium-size tomatoes,
    finely chopped
2 teaspoons sugar
¹/4 teaspoon ground cloves
3 tablespoons vegetable oil
Hot water
1 cup sweet white wine
1 tablespoon butter
Orange slices
Parsley sprigs

Wash and clean the duck, trimming away all fat. Cut the duck into portion-sized pieces, and place in a dish with a mixture of lime or lemon juice and salt to taste. Drain, and rinse the pieces.

In a large bowl, combine the onion, thyme, scallion, hot pepper, vinegar, garlic, tomatoes, sugar, and cloves. Add the duck and toss to coat each piece well. Cover and set aside for at least 2 hours. Drain off the marinade and reserve for later use.

Heat the vegetable oil in a large skillet, and sauté the pieces of duck evenly on all sides until brown, adding small amounts of hot water to prevent burning. Reduce the heat and add the reserved marinade. Taste for salt. Add the wine, cover, and simmer for 30 minutes, or until the thickest pieces can be pierced with a fork. Spread the butter over the duck, and garnish with orange slices and parsley. Serve piping hot with wild rice.

Yield: 6 servings

Baked Stuffed Fish

The Caribbean Sea is rich in fish, and each island, indeed, each cook, has special ways to bake fish. This is my recipe, one I use repeatedly; it never fails to get good reviews. It is not necessary to remove the backbone of the fish, although it makes for easier stuffing and eating.

2 tablespoons lime or lemon
  juice
Salt and freshly ground pepper
  to taste
3-pound to 4-pound fish,
  preferably red snapper,
  cleaned and scaled, backbone removed, washed,
  and ready to cook
1 small christophene (chayote),
  diced
1 cup unseasoned dried bread
  crumbs
1 medium-size onion, finely
  chopped
4 tablespoons butter, at room
  temperature
2 garlic cloves, minced
1 small fresh hot pepper,
  seeded and minced
1/2 teaspoon dried thyme
1/2 teaspoon paprika
1/4 cup vegetable oil
1 cup warm water
1 medium-size onion, sliced

In a bowl, mix together the lime or lemon juice with the salt and pepper to taste. Rub the fish with this mixture, inside and out. Set aside.

Parboil the christophene in salted water to cover for 15 minutes. Drain.

In a bowl, combine the christophene, bread crumbs, chopped onion, 2 tablespoons of the butter, the garlic, hot pepper, thyme, and paprika. Mix well. Stuff the cavity of the fish with this mixture and secure the opening by sewing or skewering. Rub the remaining 2 tablespoons butter on the outside of the fish.

Pour the vegetable oil and warm water into a baking dish large enough to hold the fish. Place the fish in the center of the dish. Bake, uncovered, in a preheated 350°F oven for about 45 minutes, basting with the liquids from time to time. About 20 minutes before serving, add the sliced onion to the liquid. Remove to a serving dish, pour the remaining liquid over the fish, and serve.

Yield: 6 servings

Court Bouillon of Red Snapper

Another entrée from the French islands, court bouillon here is not fish stock, but the sauce in which the red snappers are cooked. The fish of choice is the easily available red snapper, but any variety of fish can be used.

4 whole red snappers, about
    1¹/2 pounds each, cleaned
    and scaled
1 teaspoon dried thyme
1 small fresh hot pepper,
    seeded and minced
2 garlic cloves, minced
4 scallions, finely chopped
8 tablespoons lime juice
1 cup water
¹/4 cup olive oil
2 medium-size onions, finely
    chopped
1 cup dry white wine
3 cups water
Salt and freshly ground pepper
4 medium-sized tomatoes,
    peeled and chopped

Thoroughly wash the fish under cold water and pat dry with paper towels. Combine the thyme, hot pepper, garlic, and scallions in a small bowl. Rub the cavities of the fish well with this mixture. Then place the fish in a shallow dish and cover with 6 tablespoons of the lime juice and 1 cup water. Marinate for 1 hour. Drain and discard the marinade.

In a skillet large enough to hold the fish, heat the olive oil. Add the onions and sauté over medium heat, stirring until tender but not browned. Add the wine, 3 cups water, and salt and pepper to taste. Bring to a boil; then reduce the heat and simmer for 2 minutes. Add the fish and tomatoes. Cook, uncovered, at a gentle simmer for about 10 minutes.

To serve, remove the fish to a serving platter or individual dinner plates. Stir the remaining 2 tablespoons of lime juice into the sauce and pour over the fish.

Yield: 4 servings

Poisson en Blaff

This peppery dish of poached fish is a popular dish from the lively islands of Martinique and Guadeloupe, where it is often cooked right on the beach with freshly caught fish. Curiously, the word "blaff" is said to come from the sound the fish makes when it hits the poaching liquid in the skillet.

3 cups water
5 tablespoons lime or lemon juice
1 fresh hot pepper, seeded and crushed
4 garlic cloves, minced
2 teaspoons salt
2 (1-pound) red snappers, cleaned with heads and tails intact
1 cup dry white wine
1 large onion, finely chopped
1 whole fresh hot pepper
2 cloves
1/2 teaspoon allspice berries
1 bay leaf
1/2 teaspoon dried thyme

Combine 2 cups of the water with 4 tablespoons of the lime or lemon juice, 1 seeded and crushed fresh hot pepper, 3 of the minced garlic cloves, and the salt in a dish deep enough to hold the fish. Add the fish. Cover and marinate for 1 hour at room temperature.

Drain the fish and discard the marinade. Combine the wine, the remaining 1 cup water, onion, whole fresh hot pepper, remaining minced garlic clove, remaining 1 tablespoon lime or lemon juice, the cloves, allspice berries, bay leaf, and thyme in a large skillet. Bring to a boil, reduce the heat, and simmer for 5 minutes. Add the fish and continue to simmer for about 10 minutes.

Serve the fish with some of the poaching liquid with boiled green bananas and/or white rice and fried plantains. A vegetable salad and a bottle of Beaujolais complete the meal nicely.

Yield: a servings

Colombo de Poisson

Colombo is a type of curry unique to the French islands. It is frequently used with fish, lamb, chicken, and even pumpkin (*colombo de giromon*). My favorite colombo dish is this Curried Fish Stew, preferably made with shark, although any firm-fleshed fish will do.

4 cups water
1/2 cup dry white wine
Whole peppercorns
2 pounds fresh shark, cubed
1/4 cup peanut oil
2 small onions, finely chopped
Colombo (page 138)
1 teaspoon all-purpose flour
1 cup chicken broth
1/2 cup coconut cream
  (page 150)
2 tablespoons lime or lemon
  juice
2 tablespoons dark rum
1 scallion, chopped
Salt and freshly ground pepper

Combine the water, wine, and peppercorns in a saucepan and bring to a boil, then reduce the heat to a simmer. Add the fish and poach until opaque. Transfer the fish to a dish and discard the liquid.

Heat the oil in a large skillet over medium heat, add the onions, and sauté for 2 minutes. Stir in the Colombo and flour. Add the chicken broth, stirring occasionally until the sauce thickens. Stir in the coconut cream, lime or lemon juice, rum, scallion, and salt and pepper to taste. Stir in the fish and cook for another 5 minutes. Serve over a bed of steaming white rice.

Yield: 4 servings

Fish Fingers ▲▽▲▼▲▽▲▽▲▽▲▽▲▽▲▽▲▽▲▽

1 pound white-fleshed fish
    fillets
Salt and freshly ground pepper
1 tablespoon freshly squeezed
    lime juice
2 eggs, slightly beaten
1/2 cup milk
1 cup all-purpose flour
Vegetable oil for deep frying

Cut the fish fillets into finger-length strips and season with salt and pepper to taste and the lime juice. Combine the eggs and milk in a small bowl. Dip the fish strips in the milk, then dredge in the flour, shaking off any excess.

Heat the oil in a large skillet and fry the fish evenly until golden brown. Drain on paper towels. Serve with coleslaw, potato salad, or any vegetable salad. Be sure to sprinkle a few dashes of your favorite hot pepper sauce on the fish.

Yield: 2 servings

Run Down ▲▽▲▼▲▽▲▽▲▽▲▽▲▽▲▽▲▽▲▽

No one seems to know how this unusual Jamaican dish got its name. The closest explanation is that the coconut milk is cooked down to produce the sweet custard in this dish. The boiled green bananas suggested as an accompaniment can be peeled and added at the same time as the fish.

1 pound pickled mackerel,
    herring, or shad
2 cups fresh coconut milk
    (page 149)
1 teaspoon freshly ground
    black pepper
1 scallion, chopped
1 sprig fresh thyme
1 hot pepper, seeded and
    sliced
1 garlic clove, crushed
2 medium-size tomatoes,
    chopped
1 large onion, chopped
1 teaspoon malt vinegar

Soak the fish in cold water to cover for at least 1 hour, then wash thoroughly and remove the fins and bones. Cut the fish into 2-inch slices.

Boil the coconut milk in a heavy skillet for 15 to 20 minutes, or until a creamy top forms. Add the fish and cook for another 10 minutes. Then add all the remaining ingredients, reduce the heat, and simmer for 15 minutes. Serve piping hot with boiled green bananas.

Yield: 2 servings

Grouper Cutlets ▲ ▽ ▲▽▲▽▲ ▽ ▲ ▽ ▲ ▽ ▲ ▽ ▲ ▽

This recipe is from the Bahamas, where the fertile fishing banks teem with grouper. Sole, porgy, or flounder would also be appropriate in this recipe.

2 pounds grouper fillets (or any firm-fleshed fish)
3 tablespoons lime or lemon juice
1 teaspoon salt
1 teaspoon freshly ground black pepper
1/2 cup unseasoned dried bread crumbs
1 egg, lightly beaten
1 tablespoon milk
1/2 cup vegetable oil

Wash the fish and marinate in lime or lemon juice for at least 2 hours at room temperature. Combine the salt, pepper, and bread crumbs in a dish. Beat together the egg and milk in another dish.

Heat the oil in a skillet until it sizzles. Remove the fish from the lime or lemon juice and drain. Dip the cutlets in the egg-milk batter, drain, then coat in the bread crumbs. Place the cutlets in the hot oil and fry on both sides until golden. Drain and serve at once.

Yield: 4 servings

Steamed Grouper ▲ ▽ ▲▽▲ ▽▲▽ ▲ ▽ ▲ ▽ ▲ ▽ ▲ ▽ ▲ ▽ ▲

1/2 cup vegetable oil
2 pound grouper fillets, cut into 10inch slices
1 onion, sliced
1 green pepper, seeded and sliced
1 celery rib, chopped
1 cup sliced mushrooms
1 medium-size tomato, diced
2 cups water
1/4 cup tomato paste
Salt and freshly ground pepper
2 tablespoons all-purpose flour

Heat 1/4 cup of the oil in a medium-size skillet and add the fish. Sauté for 5 minutes, allowing 2 1/2 minutes for each side. Remove the fish from the pan and set aside.

Heat the remaining 1/4 cup oil in a medium-size skillet. Add the onion, green pepper, celery, mushrooms, and tomato and sauté for 5 minutes. Slowly pour in 1 1/2 cups of the water, then stir in the tomato paste. Cook over low heat for 5 minutes. Add salt and pepper to taste, then add the grouper and continue to cook over low heat for about 10 minutes.

Combine the remaining 1/2 cup water with the flour and mix into a paste. Stir into the sauce, cover, and cook for a few minutes until the liquid begins to bubble. Serve hot with the sauce spooned over the fish.

Yield: 2 servings

Salt Fish and Ackee

This is Jamaica's national dish, and the ackees—the essence of the dish—are the fruit of a tree that is West African in origin. The tree is found throughout the Caribbean and Central America, but only in Jamaica is the ackee cultivated as part of the country's food supply. The edible portions of the ackee are called pegs. When cooked, they resemble scrambled eggs. Ackees are available fresh or canned in Jamaica. In the States you can find it canned in Hispanic and West Indian grocery stores.

Some cooks prepare this recipe without the fish, substituting fried pork or other fried meats.

1 pound salted codfish
  (bacalao), *preferably
  boned*
*1/4 pound diced salt pork or
  6 bacon strips*
1/4 cup coconut or vegetable oil
*1 hot pepper, seeded and
  sliced*
2 scallions, chopped
*1 medium-size tomato, finely
  chopped*
1 onion, chopped
*1 (19-ounce) can ackees or
  2 dozen parboiled pegs
  (see note)*
*1/2 teaspoon freshly ground
  black pepper*
*1 green pepper, seeded and
  chopped*

Soak the codfish in cold water to cover for about 30 minutes. Drain and place the fish in 1 quart of water. Bring to a rolling boil, then drain the water. Remove any bones and skin from the codfish and flake the meat with a fork, then set it aside.

Place the salt pork or bacon in a skillet and fry until crisp in its own oil. Reduce the heat and add the coconut oil, hot pepper, scallions, tomato, and onion. Sauté until the onion is translucent.

Drain the ackees and stir into the skillet with flaked codfish. Sprinkle with the black pepper, cover, and cook over low heat for 5 minutes. Remove serving portions from the skillet with a slotted spoon to avoid the excess oil. Garnish with the sweet green pepper. Serve with boiled green bananas, roasted breadfruit slices, and dumplings.

NOTE: *To parboil pegs of ackee, place in salted water to cover in a saucepan. Bring to a boil over medium heat. Then drain and set the ackee aside until you are ready for it.*

Yield: 4 servings

Codfish au Gratin

This dish is from Puerto Rico, although similar recipes exist throughout the Caribbean. The ubiquitous dried and salted codfish is dressed up in this entrée, and the high point is the salsa.

1 pound salted codfish (bacalao), preferably boned
3 tablespoons butter
1 large onion, chopped
1 tablespoon all-purpose flour
1 garlic clove, minced
2 teaspoons tomato paste
1 bay leaf
1/2 cup dry white wine
1 cup water
1 tablespoon lemon juice
2 tablespoons sliced olives
1 tablespoon chopped fresh parsley
2 tablespoons sliced mushrooms
Salt and freshly ground pepper
2 tablespoons grated Parmesan cheese
1 medium-size potato, peeled, cooked, and slightly mashed

Soak the fish in water to cover for at least 4 hours. Remove any skin and bones and flake with a fork. Butter a 2-quart casserole with 1 tablespoon of the butter and cover the bottom with the codfish.

Heat the remaining 2 tablespoons butter in a saucepan over medium heat, add the onion, and sauté until brown. Stir in the flour and garlic, mixing well. Add the tomato paste, bay leaf, wine, water, and lemon juice. Reduce the heat and cook, stirring, until the mixture thickens. Add the olives, parsley, and mushrooms, then taste for salt and pepper. Stir and cook for 3 minutes. Remove the sauce from the heat and pour over the fish in the casserole. Sprinkle with the cheese and line the corners of the casserole with the potato.

Bake in a preheated 350°F oven for 35 minutes or until the top is golden brown. Serve with a green salad.

Yield: 4 to 6 servings

Conch Stew

Conch Stew with variations is found on all the islands. In some kitchens, the uncooked rice is added to the conch after 1½ hours of cooking. If you want to cook it this way, be sure that there is enough liquid to cook the rice.

2 pounds conch
½ cup lime or lemon juice
3 tablespoons olive oil
½ teaspoon chopped fresh
    parsley
½ teaspoon dried thyme
1 bay leaf, crumbled
1 fresh hot pepper, seeded and
    sliced
2 garlic cloves, minced
2 scallions, chopped
Salt and freshly ground pepper

Marinate the conch in the lime or lemon juice for at least 2 hours at room temperature. Drain and rinse under cold water, then pound the conch to tenderize. Cut into small pieces, cover with water in a saucepan, and cook over low heat for 2 hours.

Heat the oil in a large skillet and add the parsley, thyme, bay leaf, fresh hot pepper, garlic, scallions, and salt and pepper to taste. Sauté for 5 minutes, add the conch, cover, reduce the heat, and simmer for 10 minutes. Serve hot.

Yield: 4 servings

Conch Salad

This is one of my favorite Bahamian dishes. When I'm visiting the Bahamas, I think my trip is incomplete if I do not have this salad for lunch or as a side dish. This is virtually the same as conch cerviche served in the Yucatan and in other parts of Mexico. It is great with hot rolls and a cold beer.

1 pound conch, pounded and
    cut into small pieces
½ cup diced onions
½ cup diced cucumber
½ cup diced green pepper
½ cup diced celery
1 large tomato, peeled, seeded,
    and minced (optional)
½ cup lime or lemon juice
Salt and freshly ground pepper
    to taste
Lettuce leaves

Mix together all the ingredients, except the lettuce, and place in a covered dish to marinate for a few hours at room temperature, or overnight in the refrigerator. Serve on crisp lettuce leaves.

Yield: 4 to 6 servings

Matoutou de Crabes

With Caribbean cuisine the addition or deletions of a few ingredients can cause wars between islands. In Guadeloupe and Martinique, this recipe for crab stew comes from a Carib word, *matoutou,* meaning cooked with farina (cassava meal). The Carib word for a dish that is cooked with rice is *matété* in Guadaloupe, but for some unexplainable reason, this dish, which is cooked with rice, is properly known as *matoutou.* A remarkably similar dish is found in Tobago: Crab Pilau. In that dish, 2 tablespoons of curry powder and 1 chopped onion are sautéed with the other ingredients. And, instead of the water, 4 cups of coconut milk are used. Both versions are quite delicious.

1/4 cup olive oil
2 pounds raw crab meat,
    cleaned and chopped
1/4 cup chopped shallots
    (optional)
4 garlic cloves, minced
2 tablespoons chopped chives
1/4 teaspoon dried thyme
1 bay leaf, crumbled
1 fresh parsley sprig
2 tablespoons lime juice
1 small fresh hot pepper,
    seeded and minced
Salt and freshly ground pepper
    to taste
4 cups water
2 cups rice, white or brown

Heat the oil in a large, heavy saucepan, add the crab meat, and sauté for 5 minutes, stirring frequently to prevent sticking. Add all the remaining ingredients, except the water and rice. Sauté for 2 to 3 minutes. Pour in the water slowly, and when the liquid begins to bubble, add the rice. Cover and cook over low heat for about 20 to 40 minutes, depending on the rice, or until the liquid is absorbed. Serve hot.

Yield: 6 servings

Curried Lobster

1/4 cup vegetable oil
1 large tomato, chopped
1 onion, chopped
2 scallions, finely chopped
2 tablespoons curry powder
1 cup water
2 pounds raw lobster meat,
    chopped
Salt and pepper
2 tablespoons butter

Heat the oil in a large, heavy skillet, add the tomato, onion, scallions, and curry powder and sauté for 5 minutes. Slowly pour in the water, stir, and when the liquid starts to bubble, add the lobster meat. Cover, reduce the heat, and simmer gently for 15 minutes. Add salt and pepper to taste. Stir in the butter just before removing from the heat and serve hot with rice and a salad.

Yield: 6 servings

Deviled Lobster

Although you can make and serve this dish in individual ramekins, it is spectacular served in scallop shells. Allow 2 shells per serving.

2 pounds lobster meat, cooked
    and diced
1 cup fresh bread crumbs
2 hard-cooked eggs, chopped
2 tablespoons vegetable oil
2 scallions, finely chopped
1 large onion, finely chopped
1 medium-size tomato, finely
    chopped
1 cup milk, scalded
1 tablespoon flour
2 tablespoons lime or lemon
    juice
1/4 teaspoon hot pepper sauce
Salt and freshly ground pepper
Butter

In a large bowl, combine the lobster meat with 1/2 cup of the bread crumbs and the hard-cooked eggs. Set aside.

In a skillet, heat the oil. Add the scallions, onion, and tomato and sauté until the onion is translucent. Add to the lobster mixture.

Mix together the milk and flour, then add to the lobster with the lime or lemon juice, hot pepper sauce, and salt and pepper to taste.

In a large saucepan over low heat, cook the lobster mixture for about 10 minutes, stirring constantly. Spoon the mixture into scallop shells and sprinkle the remaining 1/2 cup bread crumbs on top. Dot with butter and bake in an oven preheated to 350°F for about 10 minutes, or until the bread crumbs begin to brown. Serve hot.

Yield: 4 to 6 servings

Rice with Shrimp and Tomatoes

Simply called Shrimp and Rice in much of the Caribbean, this dish is from the Dominican Republic, where it tastes better than any other place. Some cooks use 4 to 6 slices of bacon instead of the salt pork. And longaniza, a Dominican sausage, is sometimes chopped and added to the dish.

*1/4 cup chopped salt pork
    (2 ounces)*
1 large onion, finely chopped
3 garlic cloves, minced
*1 small fresh hot pepper,
    seeded and minced*
*4 cups chicken stock or
    3 cups water and 1 cup
    chicken stock*
2 cups rice
*2 cups tomatoes, peeled,
    seeded, and chopped*
Salt and freshly ground pepper
2 tablespoons butter
*2 pounds raw shrimp,
    cleaned, deveined, and
    chopped*
1 teaspoon dried parsley

Fry the salt pork until crisp in a large, heavy saucepan. Remove and drain on paper towels. Add the onion, garlic, and hot pepper to the pork fat and sauté for about 2 minutes. Pour in the chicken stock or water, then add the rice and tomatoes. Stir, then add salt and pepper to taste. Bring to a boil, reduce the heat, cover, and cook for about 25 minutes.

Heat the butter in a skillet, add the shrimp, and sauté for about 5 minutes. When the rice is tender and the liquid is all absorbed, add the shrimp, salt pork, and parsley, mixing thoroughly. Cover and simmer for another 5 to 10 minutes. Serve hot. Grated Parmesan cheese can be passed on the side.

Yield: 6 to 8 servings

Shrimp Curry

Prepared throughout the Caribbean, this delicious dish has innumerable variations.

1/4 cup butter
3 medium-size onions, finely chopped
1 apple or christophene (chayote), peeled and chopped
1 garlic clove, minced
2 tablespoons curry powder
3 tablespoons all-purpose flour
2 cups chicken broth
1 tablespoon lime or lemon juice
1 bay leaf
1 teaspoon whole peppercorns
1/4 teaspoon ground ginger
2 medium-size tomatoes, peeled and chopped
Salt and freshly ground pepper
2 pounds raw shrimp, cleaned and deveined

In a large, heavy skillet, melt the butter and add the onions, apple or christophene, garlic, and curry powder. Sauté for about 5 minutes. Then stir in the flour. Add the chicken broth, lime or lemon juice, bay leaf, peppercorns, ginger, tomatoes, and salt and pepper to taste. Bring to a rolling boil. Reduce the heat and simmer for about 20 minutes, stirring occasionally.

Add the shrimp, cover, and cook for about 8 minutes, or until the shrimp turns pink. Discard the bay leaf and peppercorns before serving. Serve over a bed of boiled rice with mango chutney (page 93) or use to fill six 12-inch rotis (page 141).

Yield: 6 servings

Biftek à la Créole

A true Martiniquais treat is Creole dish. A prime New York sirloin tip roast can replace the rump steak.

2 garlic cloves, crushed
2 tablespoons olive oil
1 tablespoon red wine vinegar
Salt and freshly ground pepper
3-pound rump steak or loin
    tenderloin roast
1/4 cup dark rum

Combine the garlic, olive oil, vinegar, and salt and pepper to taste in a bowl and stir well. Place the steak in a large dish and pour the marinade over it. Marinate for at least 3 hours at room temperature, occasionally turning the steak.

Drain the steak, reserving the marinade, and pat dry. Broil the steak on a rack in the broiler for about 8 minutes on each side for rare meat, basting from time to time with the reserved marinade.

Transfer the steak to a heated flame-resistant dish and pour the pan juices over it. Heat the rum in a small saucepan and pour over the steak. In an open space, away from gas or the oven, cabinets and the like, ignite the steak and let the flames go out. Slice and serve.

Yield: 6 servings

Curried Beef

Like most of the recipes with curry, this dish has its roots in East Indian cuisine.

1/4 cup vegetable oil
1 garlic clove, minced
2 sprigs chives, chopped
1 small fresh hot pepper,
    seeded and sliced (optional)
2 medium-size onions,
    chopped
1 teaspoon ground ginger
2 tablespoons curry powder
2 pounds lean beef, cut into
    1-inch cubes
2 cups water
Salt

Heat the vegetable oil in a large skillet and add the garlic, chives, pepper, onions, ginger, and curry powder. Sauté for about 2 minutes, stirring constantly. Add the cubed beef and sauté until evenly browned. Add the water and salt to taste. Reduce the heat and simmer until the meat is tender, about 1 1/2 hours. Serve with rice, mango chutney (page 93), and vegetables.

Yield: 6 servings

Pot Roast Calypso

Pot roasts are enjoyed universally. In this Caribbean version, the soy sauce and fresh hot pepper are responsible for the unique flavor.

3-pound chuck, rump, or
round roast, boneless
and tied
1 tablespoon white vinegar
2 tablespoons soy sauce
1 teaspoon dried thyme
1 tablespoon chopped fresh
parsley
1 scallion, finely chopped
1 fresh hot pepper, seeded
and mince
Salt and freshly ground pepper
2 tablespoons all-purpose flour
3 tablespoons butter
1 medium-size carrot, sliced
2 cups beef stock
1/2 cup water
2 medium-size potatoes,
peeled and sliced
1 medium-size onion, sliced

Trim any excess fat from the roast, then rub well with the vinegar and soy sauce. Combine the thyme, parsley, scallion, hot pepper, and salt and pepper to taste, and rub into the roast. Place the roast in a pan and leave at room temperature for about 2 hours.

Remove and reserve the bits of seasonings, then dust the roast evenly with the flour. Melt the butter in a large, heavy pot and brown the roast on all sides. Add the carrots and sauté quickly, then add the reserved seasonings and beef stock. Cover and simmer for about a hours, turning the roast occasionally. Add the water, and when the liquid returns to a boil, add the potatoes and onion. Cook for another 30 minutes. Remove the string from the meat before thinly slicing. Serve the meat and vegetables with the pan juices as gravy.

Yield: 6 to 8 servings

Plantain and Meat Casserole

This dish originates in Puerto Rico where it is known as *Pinon*. It is an inexpensive treat. Six ripe bananas can replace the plantains.

3 tablespoons lard or vegetable oil

3 ripe plaintains, peeled and sliced lengthwise

1 pound ground beef

Sofrito (page 137)

4 eggs

12 ounces cooked fresh, frozen, or canned string beans, drained

Heat the lard or oil in a skillet, add the plantain slices, and fry until soft and golden. Remove from the oil, drain on paper towels, and set aside.

Mix the ground beef with the Sofrito, place in the skillet, and cook over medium heat until well browned. Cover, reduce the heat, and simmer for 5 minutes. Drain off the oil.

Grease a 2-quart casserole and cover the bottom with 2 beaten eggs. Place a layer of fried plantains, then the cooked ground beef, string beans, and another layer of fried plantains. Top with the remaining 2 eggs, beaten. Bake in a preheated 350°F oven for about 30 minutes. Serve directly from the casserole for dinner or lunch.

Yield: 4 to 6 servings

Tripe and Beans

Called *mondongo* in Spanish-speaking countries, tripe is a popular meat in the islands. This recipe was created by borrowing from here and there. Honeycomb tripe, widely available, is the choice cut for this recipe.

3 pounds tripe
4 cups water
1 garlic clove, minced
1 tablespoon curry powder or
  1 tablespoon tomato paste
1/4 teaspoon whole allspice
  berries
1 sprig fresh thyme
1 large onion, chopped
1 small green pepper, seeded
  and chopped
1 cup dry or fresh baby lima
  beans or 1 (12-ounce) can,
  drained
Salt and freshly ground pepper

Thoroughly wash the tripe in cold water and trim off any fat. Cut the tripe into portion-sized pieces and place in a large saucepan with water to cover. Bring to a boil, discard the water, cover again with fresh water, and bring to a second boil. Drain.

Combine the tripe with 4 cups of fresh water and all the ingredients, except the canned or fresh lima beans (dry limas should be added now). Bring to a boil, stir, and simmer, covered, until tender, about 2 1/2 hours. Add water as needed. If canned or fresh lima beans are used, add them 15 minutes before the end of cooking time. Taste for salt and pepper before removing from the heat. Serve with rice and boiled green bananas.

Yield: 6 to 8 servings

Baked Christophenes with Beef Filling

2 large christophenes
(chayotes) (5 to 6 inches
long)
3 tablespoons butter or
margarine
1/2 pound lean ground beef
1 small onion, minced
Salt and pepper to taste
1/2 cup grated cheddar cheese
2 tablespoons unseasoned
dried bread crumbs

Cover the christophenes with water and bring to a boil in a medium-size saucepan. Reduce the heat and cook for about 30 minutes. Cool. Cut into halves lengthwise, then scoop out the fleshy seed and pulp without puncturing the skin, leaving a 1/4-inch shell. Mash the flesh well in a small bowl and reserve the shells.

Melt 2 tablespoons of the butter in a skillet over low heat. Add the beef and onion and sauté until brown, stirring occasionally. Stir in the mashed christophenes, add salt and pepper to taste, and simmer for 10 minutes. Spoon the mixture into the christophene shells, sprinkle the cheese and bread crumbs over the tops, and dot with the remaining 1 tablespoon butter or margarine. Set in a baking pan, and pour about 1/2 inch of hot water around christophenes.

Bake in a preheated 350°F oven for about 20 minutes, or until the bread crumbs are brown and the filling is set. Serve hot.

Yield: 2 to 4 servings

Kidneys with Sherry

A Caribbean favorite, kidneys are usually breakfast fare. This version is known as *Riñones con Jerez* in Puerto Rico, where the sherry adds pizzazz.

1 pound beef kidneys
1/4 cup butter
2 large onions, thinly sliced
1/4 cup all-purpose flour
1/4 teaspoon dried thyme
Salt and freshly ground pepper
1/2 cup cooking sherry or
water

Clean the kidneys by removing the skin and cutting away the fat. Wash under cold water and cut each in half lengthwise. Drain, dry with paper towels, and set aside.

Heat the butter in a skillet, add the onions, and sauté until brown. Remove the onions from the skillet and set aside.

Combine the flour, thyme, and salt and pepper to taste in a bowl. Dredge the kidneys in the mixture, then sauté in the heated butter for about 5 minutes. Add the sherry, stir, and simmer for another 2 minutes. Spoon the kidneys onto a serving dish and cover with the browned onions. Serve for breakfast, lunch, or supper. French bread or green bananas are the choice accompaniments to kidneys.

Yield: 4 servings

Oxtail Stew

3 pounds oxtails
1/2 pound carrots, sliced
1 large onion, chopped
4 cups water or 3 cups water
and 1 cup beef stock
1/4 teaspoon dried thyme
1/4 teaspoon ground allspice
2 tablespoons tomato paste
Salt and freshly ground pepper
to taste
1 bay leaf, crumbled
Flour dumplings (page 142)

Clean the oxtails, trim away any excess fat, and cut into 2-inch pieces. Combine all ingredients, except the dumplings, in a large, heavy saucepan Cover and simmer for about 2 hours. Add water if necessary. Stir, add the dumplings, and return to low heat for 20 minutes. Serve hot.

NOTE: *As an alternative to the dumplings, 1 1/2 cups large dry lima beans can be added with the other ingredients at the start of cooking. Or 1 (16-ounce) can of lima beans can be drained and added 15 minutes before the end of the cooking time.*

Yield: 6 to 8 servings

Curried Goat

Curried mutton, as goat is sometimes called, is served in Jamaica and some English-speaking islands. Young goat, or kid, is best for this dish as the meat is tender and tasty. In the French islands where lamb is usually the meat of choice, the dish, varied somewhat, is *Colombo d'Agneau.* When you use lamb, add 2 tablespoons of dark rum and 1 tablespoon of lime juice about 5 minutes before the end of the cooking time.

2 pounds goat or lamb
2 tablespoons curry powder
1 teaspoon salt
1 large onion, chopped
1 teaspoon freshly ground
   black pepper
2 tablespoons vegetable oil
2 cups water
2 small potatoes, peeled and
   diced

Prepare the meat by trimming away any fat and wiping with a paper towel. Cut into portion-sized pieces. Season by rubbing with curry powder, salt, onion, and black pepper. Allow to stand in a covered dish for at least 2 hours. Remove the onion pieces and pat dry with a towel.

Heat the oil in a skillet over a medium heat, add the meat, and sauté until it is evenly browned. Add the water, then cover the skillet, and allow the meat to cook slowly over low heat for 1 hour. Add the diced potatoes and reserved onions, and a small amount of water if needed for a thinner gravy, and simmer until the meat is fork-tender, about 45 minutes.

Serve over a bed of white rice with green bananas, or use as a filling (with any bones removed) for rotis (page 141).

NOTE: *At the same time the potatoes are added, you can stir in a tablespoon of raisins or plain yogurt for a sweet or creamy gravy.*

Yield: 6 servings

Curried Rabbit

3 tablespoons butter
3 pounds rabbit, cut into
    portion-sized pieces
2 onions, finely chopped
2 tablespoons all-purpose flour
2 tablespoons curry powder
1 green pepper, finely chopped
3 cups rabbit or chicken stock
Salt and freshly ground pepper
1 fresh hot pepper, seeded and
    minced (optional)
1 tablespoon lemon juice

Heat the butter in a large, heavy skillet, add the rabbit, and sauté until evenly browned. Remove the rabbit pieces to a saucepan and cover. In the same butter, sauté the onions for about 3 minutes. Stir in the flour, curry powder, and green pepper. Cook for 2 minutes. Add the rabbit or chicken stock and bring to a boil. Pour this mixture over the rabbit. Season to taste with salt and pepper and add the fresh hot pepper, if desired. Cover and simmer for about 2 hours.

Just before the end of the cooking time, add the lemon juice. Then taste, adjust the seasonings, and serve.

Yield: 6 servings

One Pot Rabbit

4 pounds rabbit, cut into
    portion-size pieces
Salt and freshly ground pepper
1/4 cup vegetable oil
2 medium-size onions, sliced
1 pound carrots, sliced
2 pounds sweet potatoes,
    peeled and diced
2 medium-size tomatoes,
    finely chopped
2 tablespoons all-purpose flour
2 cups rabbit or chicken stock
1 sprig fresh thyme
1 sprig fresh parsley
1 scallion, finely chopped
1 small fresh hot pepper
1 green pepper, finely chopped

Season the rabbit well with salt and pepper. Heat the oil in a large skillet, add the rabbit pieces, onions, and carrots, and sauté until the meat is browned.

Cover the bottom of a large, well-buttered, 3-quart casserole with some of the sweet potatoes, rabbit, onions, and carrots. Make layers of tomatoes, potatoes, rabbit, onions, and carrots until all is used. Sprinkle salt and pepper over each layer.

Stir the flour into the rabbit or chicken stock and pour over the casserole. Tie the thyme, parsley, scallion, and hot pepper in a piece of cheesecloth (bouquet garni) and add to the casserole. Sprinkle the green pepper on top. Cover and bake in a 350°F oven for about 2 1/2 hours. Remove the bouquet garni and serve hot.

Yield: 6 to 8 servings

Roast Pork

Roast pork is another perennial favorite, with many different versions. This is mine, using slivers of ginger in the Jamaican way. Some cooks mix $1/2$ cup of rum with the sugar and lime juice and pour the mixture over the roast about halfway through cooking.

4-pound to 4-pound leg or shoulder of pork
3 garlic cloves, crushed
1 teaspoon fresh thyme leaves
1 small onion, finely chopped
1 ounce fresh ginger, slivered
$1/2$ cup soy sauce
$1/2$ cup water
2 tablespoons brown sugar
2 tablespoons lemon juice
2 tablespoons vegetable oil
$1/2$ teaspoon hot pepper sauce
Salt and freshly ground pepper

Prepare the pork by washing in cold water, then pat dry. Make criss-cross incisions on each side of the pork, wide and deep enough to accommodate a forefinger.

In a small bowl, combine the garlic, thyme, onion, and slivers of fresh ginger. Stuff the incisions with equal amounts of the mixture.

Combine the remaining ingredients in another bowl and mix well. Rub this marinade into the pork. Place the meat in a casserole or deep dish, pour over the remaining marinade, cover, and refrigerate overnight, or for at least 4 hours, turning a few times. Leave uncovered at room temperature for an hour before cooking. Scrape away and reserve the excess marinade and seasonings from the pork and pat it dry. Wrap the pork in aluminum foil, leaving an opening at the top. Place it in a baking pan and pour the reserved marinade in through the opening. Close completely and bake in a 325°F oven for $3^1/4$ hours. Open the foil and bake uncovered for another 15 minutes, basting the pork with the pan juices. Remove the pork from the pan and pour off the juices to use as gravy. Slice and serve warm.

Yield: 6 to 8 servings

Pork Stew with Eggplant

In English-speaking countries the French *aubergines* are called garden eggs, egg-plants, or melongenes. In the Spanish-speaking islands, the eggplant is known as *berenjena*. In the French islands, where this recipe originated, this dish might be called *Daube de Porc aux Aubergines* or *Bélangère,* which usually refers to a larger variety of eggplant. Whatever the name, the pork is certainly enhanced by the dark-skinned, meaty-tasting vegetable.

2 1/2-pound pork roast, bone-
    less and tied
2 tablespoons all-purpose flour
1/3 cup peanut or other
    vegetable oil
2 bay leaves
1/2 teaspoon dried thyme
Salt and freshly ground pepper
1 cup water
2 pounds eggplant, peeled
    and cut into 1/2-inch cubes

Dust the pork roast with the flour. Heat the oil in a heavy casserole or saucepan. Add the pork and brown evenly. Add the bay leaves, thyme, salt and pepper to taste, and water. Simmer, covered, over low heat for 1 1/2 hours, or until the pork is tender. Add the cubed eggplant, cover, and cook for another 20 minutes, or until the eggplant is soft.

Slice the pork and serve on a heated platter with the eggplant.

Yield: 6 servings

Garlic Pork ▲▽▲▽▲▽▲▽▲▽▲▽▲▽▲▽▲▽▲▽▲▽

Portuguese in origin, this Christmas favorite in Guyana has found its way to many other islands. Fresh hot peppers are sometimes used for seasoning. They can be added according to your taste and tolerance.

1/4 pound garlic, chopped
1 teaspoon dried thyme
Salt and freshly ground pepper
4 pounds boneless pork leg or
*   shoulder*
1 tablespoon lime juice
2 cups white vinegar
Vegetable oil for frying

Mix the garlic and thyme together in a small bowl. Add salt and pepper to taste. Set aside.

Wash the pork well with the lime juice and dice into small cubes. Place the pork in a large saucepan, cover with water, and parboil for about 30 minutes. Remove the pork, drain, and discard the water. Rub the garlic mixture over the pork. Place the cubed pork in a large jar or casserole and pour on the vinegar to cover. Cover and refrigerate for 1 to 2 days.

Remove from container, drain, and pat dry with paper towels. Heat the oil in a deep fryer or tall saucepan and deep fry the meat until tender, about 10 to 15 minutes. Serve hot as a main course with rice and vegetables or as a snack or appetizer.

Yield: 8 servings

Chinese-Caribbean Sweet and Sour Pork

1 egg, beaten
2 tablespoons soy sauce
Salt and pepper
2 pounds pork loin, diced into
   1/2-inch cubes
1 tablespoon cornstarch
2 tablespoons malt vinegar
1/4 cup brown sugar
Approximately 1/4 cup tomato
   sauce
Vegetable oil
Flour

Combine the egg with the soy sauce and salt and pepper to taste. Add the diced pork and marinate for at least 20 minutes.

Combine the cornstarch, vinegar, sugar, and tomato sauce to taste in a saucepan and mix well. Heat quickly, stirring until the sugar dissolves. Set aside.

Preheat the oil for deep frying in a large, heavy skillet. Remove the pork from the marinade and dust with the flour. Then deep fry evenly. Drain and add to the sauce in the saucepan. Cook for about 3 minutes, stirring occasionally. Serve at once.

Yield: 6 servings

Souse

If you were to make this dish with portions of the pig's head and serve it with black pudding, a sausage made from pig's blood, you would have a traditional Barbadian treat. This recipe for pickled pig's feet is found in other Caribbean countries, and it is not as involved as the Barbadian souse, which can take some getting used to.

6 pig's feet, split lengthwise
2 garlic cloves, minced
2 tablespoons white vinegar
1 medium-size onion, finely
   chopped
2 fresh hot peppers, seeded
   and sliced
1 tablespoon lime or lemon
   juice
1 tablespoon salt
2 cups boiling water
1 green pepper, seeded and
   sliced
1 medium-size cucumber,
   peeled and sliced

In a saucepan, cover the pig's feet with cold salted water and add the garlic. Bring to a boil, reduce the heat, cover, and simmer for 2 hours. Discard the water, drain, and immerse the pig's feet in cold water.

Cut the meat from the pig's feet into small pieces and place in a large bowl. Combine the vinegar, onion, hot peppers, lime or lemon juice, and salt in another bowl. Add the boiling water and stir. Pour this pickle brine over the meat and steep overnight, or for at least 4 hours. To serve, arrange the meat on a platter with the green pepper and cucumber as a garnish.

Yield: 4 servings

Paella

What a meal! Paella was introduced to the islands by the Spanish, and this recipe is a good example of how an import is adapted to local foods and tastes. This version is Puerto Rican.

2 pounds raw chicken, cut into portion-sized pieces
1 pound raw red snapper fillet (or other white fish), cubed
1 pound raw lobster meat, chopped
1 pound raw shrimp, cleaned, deveined, and chopped
2 garlic cloves, minced
Salt
1/2 cup white wine
1/2 cup vegetable oil (olive oil is recommended)
1 bay leaf
2 tablespoons Sofrito (page 137)
4 cups water
3 cups uncooked rice
4 chorizos (Spanish sausages), sliced diagonally
6 boiled chopped clams or 1 (10-ounce) can Goya Red Clam Sauce
6 stuffed olives
1 fresh hot pepper, seeded and minced

Combine the chicken, red snapper, lobster, and shrimp in a large casserole. Season with the garlic and salt to taste, and add the white wine. Marinate for at least 2 hours (or overnight).

Heat 1/4 cup of the oil in a very large saucepan. Remove the chicken pieces from the marinade, add to the saucepan, and sauté until all sides are evenly browned. Add the bay leaf, Sofrito, and water to the saucepan; cover and bring to a boil. Simmer for 10 minutes, taste for salt, and add the rice. Cover, return to medium heat, and cook for 15 minutes.

Heat the remaining 1/4 cup oil in a skillet. Remove the fish, lobster, and shrimp from the marinade and add to the skillet. Quickly sauté for 5 minutes. Reduce the heat and add the sausages, clams or clam sauce, olives, and hot pepper and sauté for 2 to 3 minutes. Then combine the contents of the skillet with the chicken and rice, stirring well. Cover the saucepan and simmer for 5 minutes more.

Remove from the heat and serve hot with garlic bread, white wine, and a salad.

Yield: 12 servings

Callaloo

Callaloo can be traced back to the plantation days of the slaves. This recipe is a Trinidadian rendition, which is also popular in other Eastern Caribbean islands. Sometimes served with boiled dasheen slices, callaloo is often served with many other dishes on the table.

For those cooks who like oil, $1/4$ cup of cooking oil is usually added. However, I think the coconut milk is sufficiently greasy.

1/4 pound pig tails or salted beef, finely chopped
1/2 pound dasheen leaves (callaloo) or spinach leaves, finely chopped
1/2 pound fresh, frozen, or canned crab meat, finely chopped
1 onion, finely chopped
1 green pepper, seeded and chopped
1/2 pound fresh okras or 1 (10-ounce) frozen packet
Sprig fresh thyme
2 cups coconut milk (page 149)
Chives
Salt and pepper to taste

If you are using salted beef, soak overnight in water to cover, then drain and chop.

Place all the ingredients in a heavy saucepan over medium heat and bring to a boil. Stir, reduce the heat, and simmer for about 1 hour, until the okra seeds begin to turn pink. Serve with Foo-Foo (page 85).

Yield: 6 servings

Pepperpot

This is an Amerindian dish that can be traced to Guyana, where it has become a national dish. Cassareep, the main seasoning ingredient, is the syrupy residue made from boiling cassava with certain other spices. It is a very good preservative. Lore has it that because of the cassareep, pepperpots have passed hands through generations and centuries with the continual addition of fresh meats and cassareep.

1 pound oxtail, jointed
1 calf's foot, cleaned and cut into small pieces
1 pound pork loin, cut into bite-sized pieces
1 pound stewing beef, cut into bite-sized pieces
2 pounds chicken, cut into bite-sized pieces
1/2 pound salted beef, cut into bite-sized pieces
2/3 cup Cassareep (page 138)
1 fresh hot pepper
Salt

Combine all the meats in a large, heavy saucepan with enough cold water to cover. Bring to a boil, then add the cassareep and the hot pepper. Reduce the heat and simmer for about 3 hours or until all the meats are tender and a thick gravy forms. Add salt to taste. Remove the pepper before serving over a bed of white rice.

Yield: 6 to 8 servings

Salpicón

*1/2 pound cold boneless
   roasted beef, lamb, or pork,
   chopped*
*1 pound cold boneless roasted
   chicken, chopped*
*4 medium-size potatoes,
   peeled, cooked, and cubed*
1 cup chopped lettuce
*1 medium-size onion, finely
   chopped*
1 tablespoon capers
*1/2 cup pimiento-stuffed
   olives, sliced*
1 cup olive oil
1/4 cup white vinegar
Salt and freshly ground pepper

Combine the beef, lamb, or pork with the chicken, potatoes, lettuce, onion, capers, and olives in a large bowl. In
a small bowl, mix together the oil and vinegar. Pour the
dressing over the salad and toss. Add salt and pepper to
taste. Serve at room temperature.

Yield: 6 servings

Chinese Chop Suey, Caribbean Style

1 pound chicken breasts,
  boned and diced
1 pound lean pork, boned
  and diced
1 pound raw shrimp, cleaned,
  deveined, and chopped
1¹/2 teaspoons sugar
2 teaspoons cornstarch
4 tablespoons soy sauce
Salt and freshly ground pepper
2 tablespoons vegetable oil
1 christophene (chayote),
  peeled and finely chopped
¹/2 pound cabbage, shredded
3 cups finely chopped celery
2 tablespoons water
2 cups chopped fresh bean
  sprouts
¹/2 cup vegetable oil
2 medium-size onions,
  chopped
4 scallions, finely chopped
1 garlic clove, minced

In a large bowl, combine the chicken, pork, and shrimp. Add the sugar, cornstarch, 2 tablespoons of the soy sauce, and salt and pepper to taste. Mix well and set aside.

In a large saucepan, heat 2 tablespoons vegetable oil and add the christophenes, cabbage, and celery. Sprinkle the water over the vegetables. Add the bean sprouts and cook for 2 minutes. Do not overcook.

In a large, heavy saucepan or wok, heat the remaining ¹/2 cup oil until sizzling. Reduce the heat, and add chicken, pork, and shrimp. Cook, covered, for 15 minutes, stirring regularly. Add the cooked vegetables, onions, scallions, garlic, and the remaining 2 tablespoons soy sauce. Cover and cook for another 10 minutes, stirring occasionally. Serve hot.

Yield: 6 to 8 servings

RICE AND BEANS, VEGETARIAN MAIN DISHES, AND SIDE DISHES

The dishes in this chapter are interesting tidbits that run the gamut from teasers to filling entrées.

Perhaps nowhere outside of the East is rice eaten as regularly as in the Caribbean. Rice was introduced to the islands by the Asian immigrants who arrived in the nineteenth century. Today, rice is often married to a variety of legumes, producing such tasty and renowned dishes as the traditional Cuban black beans and rice and the Bahamian and Jamaican rice and pea combinations.

Legumes, the dried seeds of plants, such as beans, peas, and lentils, are staples in the versatile Caribbean cuisine. Inexpensive, with a high nutritive value, legumes are high in protein and low in cholesterol, sodium, and saturated fats.

The remainder of the recipes in this chapter are made from easily found vegetables—everyday ingredients in the culinary mosaic of the Caribbean.

Stewed Peas and Rice

There are a myriad of Caribbean recipes that employ beans or peas in stews. This dish is Jamaican, and it can be found on the menus of most households at least once every fortnight. Locally it is simply called Stew Peas. Remember that beans are called peas in Jamaica, and kidney beans are called red peas.

*1/2 pound salted beef or
   1/2 pound salted pig's tail,
   chopped*
*1/2 pound stewing beef, cut
   into bite-size pieces*
2 cups dried red kidney beans
4 cups cold water
*1 medium-size onion,
   chopped*
2 tablespoons tomato paste
1 sprig fresh thyme
*1/2 teaspoon freshly ground
   pepper*
*Flour Dumplings (page 142)
   (optional)*
2 1/2 cups water
1 tablespoon butter
1 teaspoon salt
1 1/4 cups long-grain white rice

Soak the salted meat overnight in cold water to cover. Drain and combine with the stewing beef, kidney beans, and 4 cups water in a saucepan. Cook, covered, over medium heat for 2 hours, adding additional water if needed. Then add the onion, tomato paste, thyme, and pepper. Stir and add the dumplings. Simmer for another 30 minutes while you prepare the rice.

To make the rice, bring the 2 1/2 cups water to a boil in a heavy saucepan. Add the butter and salt. Stir in the rice, cover, reduce the heat, and simmer for 20 to 25 minutes.

Fluff the rice with a fork and stir the beans before serving the two dishes.

Yield: 4 servings

Bahamian Peas and Rice

1/4 pound salt pork, diced
1 tablespoon vegetable oil
1 small onion, sliced
1/4 green pepper, seeded and
    sliced
1 celery rib, chopped
1 teaspoon dried thyme leaves
1/4 cup tomato pate
3/4 cup cooked pigeon peas
    (black-eyed peas can be
    substituted)
3 cups water
Salt and freshly ground pepper
2 cups uncooked white rice

Fry the pork in a large skillet until the fat has been released, then add the vegetable oil. Add the onion and sauté until translucent. Then add the green pepper, celery, thyme, and tomato paste. Reduce the heat, cover, and simmer for 5 minutes. Add the peas and cook for another 5 minutes.

Transfer the pea mixture to a saucepan and add the water and salt and pepper to taste. Bring to a boil, add the rice, and stir. Reduce the heat when the water returns to a boil. Cook, uncovered, for about 25 minutes, or until the liquid is absorbed. This is usually served as a side dish.

Yield: 6 servings

Beans and Rice Cubano

Here the renowned black turtle beans, famous in Cuban cuisine, are used in my favorite recipe, *Habichuelas y Arroz Cubano*. In the U.S., this dish is sometimes called Cuban Moors and Christians. It is frequently served as a side dish.

2 tablespoons olive oil
1 green pepper, seeded and
    chopped
1 garlic clove, minced
2 cups cooked black beans or
    1 (16-ounce) can, drained
1/4 teaspoon dried oregano
1 tablespoon white vinegar
2 pimientos, minced
Salt and freshly ground pepper
3 cups cooked rice

Heat the oil in a skillet, add the green pepper and garlic, and sauté for about 3 minutes. Stir in the beans, oregano, vinegar, and pimientos. Add salt and pepper to taste. Reduce the heat, cover, and simmer for 5 minutes. Spoon over cooked rice and serve.

Yield: 4 servings

Jamaican-Style Rice and Peas

This is my wife's recipe, and I confess, she makes this better than I do. Rice and peas are great with fish, chicken, or meat—it's a Jamaican Sunday must. The coconut milk gives this dish a sweet flavor. If you are new to the flavors of Caribbean cooking, this humble dish may strike you as exotic.

1¹/2 cups dried red kidney
* beans*
1 garlic clove, crushed
4 cups water
Salt
2 cups coconut milk
* (page 149)*
Freshly ground pepper
1 scallion, chopped
1 sprig fresh thyme
1 fresh hot pepper
2 cups uncooked rice

Combine the kidney beans, garlic, water, and salt to taste in a saucepan. Cook, covered over medium heat until tender, about 2 hours. Add the coconut milk, freshly ground pepper to taste, scallion, thyme, and whole fresh pepper. Bring to a boil, remove the hot pepper. Then add the rice and stir. Return to a boil, cover, reduce the heat, and simmer for 25 minutes, or until all the liquids have been absorbed. Serve hot as a side dish.

NOTE: *A 16-ounce can of red kidney beans can be substituted for the dried beans. Since they are already cooked, drain the beans and combine with 3 cups of water. Add all the ingredients except the rice. Bring to a boil, reduce the heat, and simmer for S minutes. Add the rice and stir with a fork. Bring to a boil, reduce the heat, and cook for about 20 minutes, or until all the liquids are absorbed.*

Yield: 6 servings

Refried Beans with Cheese

Called *Habichuelas Fritas con Queso* in Spanish-speaking islands, this recipe makes clever use of the speckled legume, pinto beans, found in many chili dishes and burritos. Refried beans are not actually refried but well-fried. Pinto beans, kin to kidney beans, turn a reddish hue after cooking.

1/4 cup vegetable oil
1 onion, finely chopped
1 garlic clove, minced
1/2 teaspoon chili powder
2 cups cooked pinto beans or
*   1 (16-ounce) can, drained*
Salt and freshly ground pepper
1/4 cup shredded cheddar cheese

Heat the oil in a large skillet, add the onion, garlic, and chili powder, and sauté over low heat until the onion is translucent. Add the beans by the tablespoon and mash into a paste until all are used. Mix well. Add salt and pepper to taste and sprinkle the shredded cheese on top. Serve as a side dish.

Yield: 4 servings

Seasoned Rice

1/4 pound salt beef or pork fat
*   back, diced*
4 cups water
1 medium-size carrot, diced
1 scallion, finely chopped
1/4 up shredded cabbage
1 small (about 1/2 pound)
*   eggplant, peeled (optional)*
*   and died*
2 cups uncooked rice
1/4 teaspoon dried thyme
1 small onion, finely chopped
1 large tomato, finely chopped
1/2 small fresh hot pepper,
*   seeded and minced*
Salt
1 tablespoon butter

In a large saucepan, soak the salt beef overnight in cold water to cover. Drain off the water. Add 4 cups of fresh water and cook over medium heat for about 30 minutes. Add the carrot and scallion, cook for 10 minutes. Then add the cabbage, eggplant, and rice. Reduce the heat, then add the thyme, onion, tomato, and hot pepper. Taste for salt, add the butter, cover, and cook over low heat for about 25 minutes, or until the water is completely absorbed. Serve hot as a main dish or side dish.

Yield: 6 to 8 servings

Alu Curry

A great vegetarian meal, this potato curry is found throughout the Caribbean where there are large concentrations of East Indians. It is also used as filling for rotis (page 141) with the potatoes slightly mashed.

1/4 cup coconut oil (page 150)
2 garlic cloves, minced
2 tablespoons curry powder
2 pounds potatoes, peeled and sliced
Slices of green mango, peeled (optional)
1 cup water
Salt

Heat the coconut oil in a large skillet and fry the garlic until golden, stirring constantly. Remove the garlic from the oil and discard. Add the curry powder to the oil and sauté for 5 minutes, stirring constantly. Add the potatoes, mango, water, and salt to taste. Reduce the heat, cover, and simmer until the potatoes are tender, about 15 minutes. Serve as a lunch, supper, or snack.

Yield: 4 servings

Garbanzo Fritters

2 cups garbanzo beans, cooked, or 1 (16-ounce) can, drained
1 egg, beaten
1 garlic clove, minced
1/2 teaspoon dried oregano
1 teaspoon chopped fresh parsley
Salt to taste
2 tablespoons all-purpose flour
1/4 teaspoon baking powder
Vegetable oil for deep frying

In a large bowl or food processor, mash the beans into a paste. Add the egg, seasonings, flour, and baking powder and mix well.

Heat the vegetable oil in a skillet, gently drop in the bean mixture by the tablespoon, and fry until golden brown. Drain on paper towels. Serve warm with any meat or fish dish.

Yield: 18 fritters

Sweet Potato Balls

The sweet potato, or *batata*, is as widely used in the Caribbean as the white potato is used in the States. This tasty side dish will appeal to those with a sweet tooth.

1 pound sweet potatoes, cooked and mashed
1 to 2 tablespoons butter
1 egg, beaten
1 medium-size onion, finely chopped
Pinch salt
1 tablespoon all-purpose flour
1/2 teaspoon chopped fresh parsley
2 tablespoons milk
Unseasoned dried bread crumbs
Vegetable oil for frying (about 1/4 cup)

Mix together all the ingredients, except the bread crumbs and oil. Form into small balls (use about 2 teaspoons of the mixture for each) and dredge in the bread crumbs. Heat the vegetable oil and fry the balls evenly until golden brown. Drain on paper towels and serve warm.

Yield: 18 balls

Baked Green Bananas

6 green (unripe) bananas, cooked (see Glossary) and mashed
2 tablespoons butter or margarine, at room temperature
1 small fresh hot pepper, seeded and minced
1 scallion, finely chopped
1/2 teaspoon dried thyme
1 cup milk
1 small onion, chopped
1 tablespoon fresh parsley leaves
Salt

Cream the bananas with the butter until smooth, then add the hot pepper, scallion, thyme, and milk. Stir, then add the onion, parsley, and salt to taste, mixing well. Turn into a well-buttered 2-quart casserole, and bake in a preheated 350°F oven for about 20 minutes, or until the top is brown. Serve hot as a side dish directly from the casserole.

Yield: 6 servings

Green Banana Salad

2 tablespoons white wine
   vinegar
2 tablespoons dry mustard
1 garlic clove, minced
1/2 cup olive oil
Salt and pepper
4 green (unripe) bananas,
   peeled, cooked (see Glossary), and sliced diagonally
2 carrots, peeled and shredded
1 medium-size tomato,
   peeled, seeded, and
   chopped
1 medium-size cucumber,
   peeled, seeded, and
   chopped
1 ripe avocado, peeled and
   sliced
1 cup diced celery
Lettuce leaves

In a small bowl, combine the vinegar, mustard garlic, olive oil, and salt and pepper to taste. Mix well.

In a large bowl, combine the bananas, carrots tomato, cucumber, avocado, and celery. Toss, then pour the dressing over the vegetables, and toss again. Line a salad bowl with the lettuce leaves and fill with the salad. Serve at room temperature.

Yield: 6 to 8 servings

Sweet Bananas

From Puerto Rico comes *Guineos en Dulce,* an unusual use of ripe bananas. Although it is served as a vegetable, it is almost as sweet as a dessert. For those with a sweet tooth, this recipe is worth the effort.

1/4 cup butter
6 large ripe bananas, peeled
1/4 cup brown sugar
1 teaspoon cinnamon
1/4 cup dry sherry
Dash lime juice

Melt the butter in a large saucepan over medium heat. Add the bananas and heat through, turning frequently. Sprinkle with the sugar and cinnamon, and stir until the sugar is dissolved. Increase the heat, add the sherry and lime juice. Boil for 2 minutes. Serve hot with any main course of meat or fish.

Yield: 6 servings

Fried Plantains in Butter ▲▽▲▽▲▽▲▽▲▽▲▽▲▽

The ripe plantain is a staple in Caribbean kitchens.

3 very ripe plantains
¹/4 cup butter
1 tablespoon coconut oil
  (page 150)
1 tablespoon lemon juice
Sugar

Peel the plantains and cut diagonally in halves, then slice the halves lengthwise so each plantain yields 4 slices, or simply slice on the diagonal to make 1-inch pieces.

Heat the butter and coconut oil in a heavy skillet. Add the plantain slices and fry for about 4 minutes on each side, lifting with a spatula from time to time to prevent sticking. Drain on paper towels. Place on a serving dish and sprinkle with lemon juice and sugar. Serve warm with any meat or fish dish, allowing 2 or 3 slices per serving.

Yield: 4 to 6 servings

Foo-Foo ▲▽▲▽▲▽▲▽▲▽▲▽▲▽▲▽▲▽

This simple dish of pounded plantain is eaten primarily in the southeastern Caribbean, but it finds its origin in West Africa, where cassava and yam are also pounded into small balls that are called foo-foo.

3 green plantains
3 tablespoons butter
  (optional)
Salt

Boil the plantains in their skins in water to cover for about 30 minutes, or until tender. Peel and chop into small pieces. Pound in a mortar until smooth or puree in a food processor. Add the butter and salt to taste, mixing well. Sprinkle with water to moisten if too dry, then form into small balls and keep warm to serve with soups and stews.

Yield: 6 servings

Cheesy Breadfruit

Move over mashed potatoes! This side dish from Barbados is well worth a try.

2 pounds fresh breadfruit or
   1 (19-ounce) can
1/4 cup grated cheddar cheese
3 tablespoons butter
1/4 cup milk
2 eggs, separated
1 green pepper, seeded and
   finely chopped
1 medium-size onion, finely
   chopped
Salt and freshly ground pepper

Peel the fresh breadfruit, cut lengthwise, and remove the core. Slice lengthwise or cut into chunks. Place in cold salted water to cover for about 30 minutes. Discard the water, replace with fresh water to cover, bring to a boil, and boil for about 20 minutes, or until tender. Mash as you would potatoes. If you are using canned breadfruit, follow the directions on the can for cooking, then mash.

In a bowl, combine the mashed breadfruit with the cheese, 2 tablespoons of the butter, and the milk. Beat the egg yolks well and add to the breadfruit. Mix thoroughly, then add the green pepper, onion, and salt and pepper to taste. Whisk the egg whites until stiff, and fold gently but thoroughly into the mixture.

Pour into a well-buttered 2^1/2-quart casserole and bake in a preheated 350°F oven for 30 minutes, or until the top is golden. Dot with the remaining 1 tablespoon butter and serve hot from the casserole with any meat or fish dish.

Yield: 6 to 8 servings

Breadfruit Chips ▲▽▲▽▲▽▲▽▲▽▲▽▲▽▲▽▲▽▲▽▲▽

1 fresh breadfruit, about
    1¹/2 pounds, or 1 (19-
    ounce) can
Vegetable oil for deep frying
Grated Parmesan cheese
Salt

Peel the fresh breadfruit, slice in half, and core. Cut into
¹/4-inch slices. Place the breadfruit slices in salted water
to cover for at least 1 hour. Drain and dry on paper towels. If you use canned breadfruit, simply cut in ¹/4-inch
slices and pat dry.

Heat the vegetable oil in a large, heavy skillet, add the
breadfruit, and fry on both sides until golden brown.
Drain on paper towels and sprinkle with grated cheese
and salt. Serve hot as a vegetable with any meat or fish
dish. The chips can be made in advance and reheated.

Yield: 6 to 8 servings

Bhagi ▲▽▲▽▲▽▲▽▲▽▲▽▲▽▲▽▲▽▲▽▲▽▲▽

Bhagi is also the name of a type of Chinese spinach. Here I substitute the more familiar
spinach.

2 tablespoons vegetable oil
1 medium-size onion, finely
    chopped
1 garlic clove, minced
1 small sweet red pepper,
    seeded and chopped
¹/2 pound spinach leaves,
    chopped
Salt

Heat the vegetable oil in a medium-size skillet. Add the
onion, garlic, and sweet pepper and sauté for about 3 minutes. Add the spinach and salt to taste, cover, reduce the
heat, and steam over low heat for about 10 minutes, or
until the spinach leaves are tender. Serve hot as a side dish.

Yield: 4 servings

Stewed Eggplant

Since coconut oil is a partially saturated fat, you may want to substitute another oil, such as corn. You will, however, be sacrificing the authentic taste of this dish.

1/2 cup coconut oil (page 150)
1 large onion, chopped
3 garlic cloves, minced
2 medium-size eggplants,
  peeled and thinly sliced
3 large tomatoes, peeled,
  seeded, and chopped
1/2 teaspoon chopped fresh
  parsley
1 teaspoon white vinegar
Salt

Heat the oil in a skillet, add the onion and garlic, and sauté for 3 minutes. Add the eggplants, tomatoes, parsley leaves, vinegar, and salt to taste. Cover and cook over low heat for about 40 minutes. Serve hot as a side dish.

Yield: 6 servings

Cou-Cou

Cou-cou means side dish, and although it is chiefly served as an accompaniment to fish—especially flying fish in Barbados—it can be served with other fish and meat dishes.

3 cups water
12 small young okras
3 cups boiling water
1 small fresh hot pepper,
  seeded and minced
Salt
2 cups yellow cornmeal
3 cups water
2 tablespoons butter

Remove the stems and slice the okras diagonally into 1/4-inch rings. In a heavy saucepan, bring the water to a boil. Add the okra, hot pepper, and salt to taste. Boil for about 10 minutes.

Meanwhile, sift the cornmeal into a bowl and add the remaining 3 cups cold water. Mix well.

Remove the saucepan from heat and combine the okras and cooking liquid with the cornmeal mixture. Return to medium heat and stir frequently until the mixture is smooth and thick. Turn out onto a platter and spread the butter on top. Serve hot.

Yield: 6 servings

Stewed Okra

Annatto in lard, a key ingredient in this dish, is available in Hispanic grocery stores as *manteca de achiote*.

2 tablespoons annatto in lard
 or paprika
2 ounces boiled ham, diced
1 ounce salt pork, diced
1 small onion, chopped
2 small tomatoes, chopped
1 teaspoon ground coriander
2 green peppers, seeded and
 chopped
3 cups water
1/4 cup tomato sauce
2 medium-size potatoes,
 peeled and diced
1 pound fresh okras, chopped,
 or 2 (10-ounce) frozen
 packages

In a large saucepan, combine the annatto in lard or paprika, ham, and salt pork. Fry over high heat for 3 minutes, stirring to prevent burning. Add the remaining ingredients and bring to a boil. Reduce to medium heat, cover, and cook for 30 minutes. Uncover and cook for another 15 minutes. Serve hot as a side dish with meat or fish.

Yield: 6 servings

SALSAS AND CHUTNEYS

Salsa, roughly translated from Spanish, means sauce. In the Caribbean the name is especially appropriate, for many of the spicy-hot sauces and relishes will make those unaccustomed to hot foods do a jig that is reminiscent of the Latin dance also called salsa.

Most Caribbean salsas are pepper-based and fiery hot. Caribbean people take enormous pleasure in hot foods. Chili peppers are in salsas, cooked in foods, or freshly cut to accompany morsels of food. Some, like the fire-eaters who accompany limbo dancers and balladeering calypsonians, actually eat raw peppers as an appetizer to meals. This practice, however, is not for the timid, for you will truly burn.

As peppers are numerous in their varieties, so are pepper sauces—each country and household has a preference. In the Caribbean, the Scotch bonnet is a commonly used variety of chili pepper. Scotch bonnets can be found in stores that cater to Caribbean immigrants. The milder, but more readily available jalapeño makes an acceptable substitute. The important thing to remember is that if your constitution for hot peppers is not strong, core each pepper and discard the seeds, which carry much of the heat. Although the skins retain some heat, they are less ferocious than the seeds. Also, be sure to thoroughly wash your hands as well as any utensils that have been in contact with the pepper.

Some dishes, especially those containing seafood, are absolutely lost without some coaxing from the master spice—pepper—but proceed with caution or risk the devil's fire.

Creole Tomato Sauce

Called *Salsa Criolla Cocida,* this is one of many similar sauces from the Dominican Republic, where tomatoes are heavily employed in cooking.

1/4 cup olive oil
1 onion, finely chopped
1 large tomato, peeled, seeded, and chopped
1 fresh hot pepper, seeded and minced
Salt and freshly ground pepper
1 tablespoon vinegar

Heat the oil in a skillet, add the onion, and sauté until soft. Add the tomato, hot pepper, and salt and pepper to taste. Stir until the sauce combines and is thick. Stir in the vinegar and cook for another 2 minutes. Serve warm or cold with meat or fish.

Yield: 1 cup

Hot Pepper Sauce

This recipe is mine but closely resembles many other homemade and even commercial blends called crushed peppers. It is used as a seasoning for meat and fish dishes and set on the table as a condiment to go with cooked meats and fish. For those with tolerance for hot peppers, the seeds can remain.

1¹/2 cups white vinegar
6 allspice berries, crushed
2 dozen fresh hot red peppers, seeded and stems removed
1/4 teaspoon annatto, crushed
1/2 teaspoon salt
2 medium-size onions, finely chopped
2 large tomatoes, finely chopped
2 garlic cloves, crushed

Bring the vinegar and allspice berries to a boil in a saucepan. Combine the peppers, annatto, salt, onions, tomatoes, and garlic in an electric blender or food processor and puree. Pour in the vinegar and liquefy. Cool, pour into a 16-ounce bottle, and refrigerate.

Yield: 2 cups

Sauce Chien

Sauce Chien (or *Sauce Chienne* as it is sometimes spelled) translates as Dog Sauce. It is a fiery hot French-Caribbean condiment that is served cold with seafood and poultry. This particular version is somewhat milder than the palate-numbing relish that is found on many tables in its homeland.

1 cup vegetable oil
1/4 cup vinegar
3 onions, finely chopped
1 garlic clove, crushed
1 small fresh hot pepper, chopped
2 tablespoons capers
1/2 teaspoon dried thyme
1/2 teaspoon dried parsley
1 bay leaf, crumbled
Salt and freshly ground pepper to taste

Combine all the ingredients in a bowl and mix well. Cover and refrigerate overnight. Pass at the table with fish and poultry dishes.

Yield: 1 cup

Trinidad Mango Chutney

Serve this condiment with any curry dish from Trinidad.

1 green (unripe) mango, peeled, seeded, and chopped
4 sprigs fresh parsley, chopped
1 fresh hot pepper, seeded and chopped
1/2 teaspoon sugar
1/4 teaspoon salt

Combine all the ingredients, mash, and blend into a paste. Serve at once, or store tightly covered in the refrigerator.

Yield: 3/4 cup

Souscaille

Souscaille is a simple variation of mango chutney. This recipe is from Martinique. It was carried there by indentured Hindu workers in the nineteenth century. Although called a chutney, it is actually served as an appetizer.

2 green (unripe) mangoes, peeled, seeded, and thinly sliced
3 garlic cloves, crushed
1 large fresh hot pepper, seeded and minced
1¹/2 cups water
¹/2 cup lime or lemon juice
Salt and freshly ground pepper to taste

Combine all the ingredients in a bowl and marinate for at least 1 hour. Discard the liquid and serve or refrigerate in a tightly covered container.

Yield: 1 cup

Papaya Chutney

Hot East Indian condiments of fruits and peppers, chutneys are served as a relish, often with curries or cold meats. This is my variation. Some cooks prefer to use very green, unripe papayas, but I prefer riper fruit. A partially ripe papaya will be green flecked with yellow and will feel hard to the touch. Raisins can be added if desired.

2 cups diced partially ripe papaya
¹/2 cup sugar
1 small christophene (chayote), peeled and diced
1 tablespoon ground ginger
¹/2 cup malt vinegar
1 medium-size onion, finely chopped
1 teaspoon salt
1 large sweet green pepper, seeded and finely chopped
1 fresh hot pepper, seeded and chopped
1 cup water

Combine all the ingredients in a saucepan and simmer gently for 45 minutes, stirring constantly Remove from the heat, cool, and pour into a 30-ounce glass jar. Store for later use. Serve with meat and chicken.

NOTE: *To make mango chutney, substitute diced partially ripe mango for the papaya and proceed as above.*

Yield: About 4¹/2 cups

DESSERTS, PASTRIES, AND BREADS

The abundance of unusually rich, succulent fruits and vegetables in the sunny Caribbean has resulted in an array of unforgettable breads, pastries, and desserts. With few exceptions, most of these recipes—tasty and simple—contain indigenous island staples, such as banana, coconut, and mango.

Flans and custards and the use of jellies and creams in such recipes as Floating Islands and Pineapple Mousse reflect a European influence. Other desserts are heavy-textured "poor folks" fare, reflecting a heritage of simple rural lifestyles. The heavy-bodied breads and Sweet Potato Pudding began as plantation goodies for African slaves on the islands; they survive today despite the desire for slim waistlines.

Modern equipment and shopping practices have allowed a universal favorite—ice cream—to be bought in supermarkets and ice cream parlors or made quickly and easily in home ice cream makers. I can remember the homemade ice cream that was a Sunday dessert treat when I was a child. The simple ice creams and sherbets presented here have not tried to improve on the old tried and true methods; they require no more than a freezer, ingredients, and desire. With the year-round availability of fresh Caribbean fruits, deliciously rich combinations are possible. The fresh soursop, or *guanábana,* may prove somewhat difficult to locate, but frozen pulp or canned nectar are available wherever Caribbean foods are sold.

With the exception of the mousses, some tarts, and the ice creams, few of these recipes are likely to be found at Caribbean hotels, which tend to offer familiar foods for their guests. And, although many households still prepare breads and puddings, especially for festive occasions, a traveler to the islands stands the best chance of finding these dishes at small local restaurants. Or better still, try some in your own kitchen.

Banana Ice Cream

This dessert is from the tiny island of Grenada.

4 eggs
1/2 cup sugar
2 cups milk, scalded
1 1/4 teaspoons vanilla extract
1/4 teaspoon ground nutmeg
4 very ripe bananas, peeled
   and mashed

Combine the eggs and sugar and beat lightly. Stir in the scalded milk and pour the mixture into the top half of a double boiler set over hot water. Cook, stirring constantly, until the custard thickens and coats the spoon. Cool, stir in the vanilla and nutmeg, and combine with the mashed bananas in an electric blender or food processor. Puree, pour into a shallow pan, cover, and freeze for about 2 hours in the freezer compartment of your refrigerator. Remove from the freezer, beat well, and return to the freezer until set. Or freeze in an ice cream maker according to the manufacturer's directions.

Yield: 8 servings

Banana Sherbet

1 1/2 cups milk
1 tablespoon unflavored
   gelatin
3 very ripe bananas, peeled
   and sliced
3/4 cup light corn syrup
1 tablespoon freshly squeezed
   lemon juice

Pour the milk into a saucepan. Sprinkle the gelatin over the milk and cook over low heat, stirring, until gelatin dissolves.

Puree the bananas in a food processor or electric blender. Pour in the milk mixture, corn syrup, and lemon juice. Blend until smooth. Pour the mixture into a shallow pan, cover, and freeze for about 2 hours in the freezer compartment of your refrigerator. Spoon into a bowl and beat at low speed until smooth. Pour into the pan and freeze again until firm. Or freeze in an ice cream maker according to the manufacturer's directions.

Yield: 6 to 8 servings

Coconut Ice Cream

When I was a boy in Jamaica, homemade coconut ice cream was sold from large hand-driven ice cream freezers at country fairs. This tasty and easy-to-prepare dessert tastes just like that ice cream I so vividly remember.

4 eggs, beaten
$^1/2$ cup sugar
2 cups milk, scalded
$^1/2$ teaspoon almond extract
1 cup heavy cream
1 cup rich coconut milk
   (page 149)
$^1/2$ cup shredded coconut
2 egg whites, beaten stiff

Combine the eggs and sugar and beat lightly. Stir in the scalded milk and pour the mixture into the top half of a double boiler set over hot water. Cook, stirring constantly, until the custard thickens and coats the spoon. Cool and stir in the almond extract.

Combine the heavy cream, coconut milk, and coconut. Add to the custard. Fold in the beaten egg whites. Pour into a shallow pan, cover, and freeze for about 2 hours in the freezer compartment of your refrigerator. Remove from the freezer, beat well, and return to the freezer until frozen. Or freeze in an ice cream maker according to the manufacturer's directions.

Yield: 8 servings

Papaya Sherbet

1/2 cup milk
1 tablespoon unflavored
   gelatin
3 cups peeled and diced ripe
   papaya
1 cup light corn syrup
1 tablespoon freshly squeezed
   lemon juice
1/4 cup sweetened condensed
   milk (optional)

Pour the milk into a saucepan. Sprinkle the gelatin over the milk. Cook over low heat, stirring, until the gelatin dissolves.

Puree the papaya in a food processor or electric blender. Pour in the milk mixture, corn syrup, and lemon juice. Blend until smooth. Pour the mixture in a shallow pan, cover, and freeze for about 2 hours in the freezer compartment of your refrigerator. Spoon into a bowl and beat at low speed until smooth. Pour into the pan and freeze again until firm. Or freeze in an ice cream maker according to the manufacturer's directions.

NOTE: *After beating the sherbet mixture for a second time and returning it to the freezer pan, I have experimented with parting a groove in a spiral pattern about 1/2 inch deep in the mixture—not quite to the bottom of the pan—and pouring in the sweetened condensed milk. The milk perks up the flavor of the papaya and adds to the visual appeal of the dessert.*

Yield: 6 to 8 servings

Mango Ice Cream

The mango, a ubiquitous Caribbbean fruit with dozens of varieties, makes a delicious ice cream. It's a bit messy to extract the fruit, but the pulp and nectar concentrates are available in many supermarkets.

4 eggs
3/4 cup sugar
2 cups milk, scalded
1/2 teaspoon vanilla extract
1 cup mango pulp or puree
Dash lime juice

Combine the eggs and sugar and beat lightly. Stir in the scalded milk. Pour the mixture into the top half of a double boiler set over hot water. Cook, stirring constantly, until the custard thickens and coats the spoon. Cool and stir in the vanilla.

Combine the custard with the mango pulp or puree and lime juice and stir well. Pour the mixture into a shallow pan and freeze for about 2 hours in the freezer compartment of your refrigerator. Remove from the freezer, beat well, and return to freezer until frozen. Or pour the mixture into an ice cream maker and freeze according to the manufacturer's directions.

Yield: 6 to 8 servings

Pineapple Ice Cream

4 eggs
1 cup sugar
2 cups milk, scalded
1 cup evaporated milk
1/2 teaspoon vanilla extract
1 cup thoroughly crushed unsweetened canned or fresh pineapple

Combine the eggs and sugar and beat lightly. Stir in the scalded milk and evaporated milk. Pour into the top half of a double boiler set over hot water. Cook, stirring constantly, until the custard thickens and coats the spoon. Cool and stir in the vanilla.

Add the pineapple to the custard. Puree in an electric blender or food processor. Pour into a shallow pan and freeze for about 2 hours in the freezer compartment of your refrigerator. Remove, beat well, and return to the freezer until frozen. Or pour the mixture into an ice cream maker and freeze according to the manufacturer's directions.

Yield: 6 to 8 servings

Soursop Ice Cream

Another delicious fruit from the Caribbean, soursop, or *guanábana* as it is called by the Spanish, is often peeled and eaten out of hand. Or it is made into desserts like this one. If the fresh spiny-skinned fruit is available, peel it and crush the cottony flesh, removing all seeds. Pour 1 1/2 cups of hot water over the pulp and allow it to stand for 1 hour. Pass through a sieve and use the resulting liquid in the recipe. The pump and the nectar can be found in West Indian and Hispanic grocery stores.

2 cups soursop nectar
1/4 cup sugar
1 (10 1/2-ounce) can sweetened condensed milk
2/3 cup evaporated milk

Combine all the ingredients in a bowl and stir well. Pour into a shallow pan, cover, and freeze for about 2 hours in the freezer compartment of your refrigerator. Remove from the freezer, beat well, and return to freezer until frozen. Or freeze in an ice cream maker according to the manufacturer's directions.

Yield: 6 to 8 servings

Rum Cream Supreme

Variations of this old-time Jamaican favorite abound in the islands.

2 cups milk
1 cup sugar
2 tablespoons unflavored
gelatin
3 egg yolks, beaten lightly
2 tablespoons custard powder
or 1 tablespoon cornstarch
mixed with about 1/4 cup
water to form a paste
3 ounces dark rum
1 cup whipped cream

Combine the milk and sugar in a saucepan. Sprinkle the gelatin over the milk. Cook over a low heat, stirring constantly, until the gelatin is dissolved. Add the beaten egg yolks to the mixture and cook for about 10 minutes, stirring constantly. Stir in the custard powder or cornstarch paste and cook until creamy. Place the saucepan in icy cold water and stir until cool, then add the rum and fold in the whipped cream. Transfer to a bowl and set in the freezer compartment of your refrigerator for about 30 minutes. Then serve at once.

Yield: 6 servings

Floating Islands

The Caribbean version of Floating Islands is a delicious combination of custard and guava jelly. If you can't find guava jelly in your local supermarket, substitute any fruit preserve.

3 eggs, separated
1/2 cup sugar
2 cups light cream, scalded
1 teaspoon vanilla extract
3 tablespoons guava jelly, at
*   room temperature*

Combine the egg yolks with the sugar and beat until light and lemon colored. Slowly pour the scalded cream into the egg mixture, beating constantly. Place over hot water in the top half of a double boiler and cook over low heat, stirring constantly, until thick enough to coat a spoon. Cool, stir in the vanilla, then pour into a bowl and refrigerate.

Beat the egg whites until stiff. Fold the guava jelly into the egg whites and drop gently on the custard to form peaks or islands. Chill and serve.

Yield: 6 servings

Guava Delight

For extra punch, top this dessert with strawberries, cherries, or any combination of fresh or preserved whipped cream.

3/4 cup sugar
1 cup water
1 tablespoon unflavored
*   gelatin*
1 tablespoon lemon juice
1 cup guava pulp (about
*   6 medium-size guavas)*
2 egg whites

Combine the sugar and 3/4 cup of the water in a saucepan. Cook over low heat, stirring constantly, to dissolve the sugar.

Sprinkle the gelatin over the remaining 1/4 cup water and let it soften. Then stir it into the syrup until it dissolves. Cool.

Combine the lemon juice and guava pulp, add to the syrup, and beat well. Chill until thick. Beat the egg whites until stiff and fold them into the guava mixture gently but thoroughly. Pour into a 9-inch mold or serving bowl and chill until set.

Yield: 6 to 8 servings

Flan de Queso

This creamy Cheese Custard is a Puerto Rican recipe. It is especially beautiful when topped with fresh fruit, such as strawberries.

1 cup granulated sugar
2 (8-ounce) packets cream cheese, at room temperature
6 eggs
1 (14-ounce) can sweetened condensed milk
1 cup milk
Salt
Sugar
1 teaspoon vanilla extract

Caramelize 1 cup of sugar by placing it in a round 9-inch aluminum mold and cooking over medium heat, stirring constantly with a wooden spoon until the sugar liquefies and turns brown. Remove from heat, rotate to coat the sides and bottom of the mold, and cool.

Whip the cream cheese in an electric blender or food processor. Add the eggs, then the condensed milk and blend. Combine the cream cheese mixture with the milk, salt and sugar to taste, and vanilla extract. Mix well. Pour the mixture into the mold with the caramelized sugar.

Place the mold in a larger pan with about an inch of hot water poured around. Bake in preheated 350°F oven for about 1¹/4 hours. Remove from oven, cool, and refrigerate. Invert onto a deep-sided dish before serving.

Yield: 6 to 8 servings

Pineapple Custard

Called *Flan de Piña* in the Spanish islands, variations of this dessert show up wherever pineapple is abundant, as in Puerto Rico. It is delicious served plain or with a dollop of whipped cream or vanilla ice cream.

8 eggs
4 egg yolks
1/4 cup water
2 cups sugar
2 cups unsweetened fresh or
    bottled pineapple juice

Lightly whisk the eggs and egg yolks, and allow to stand for about 1 hour.

In a heavy saucepan, combine the water with 1/2 cup of the sugar and boil for about 5 minutes, stirring constantly until the sugar is completed dissolved and turns brown. Pour into a 2-quart mold to cover the bottom.

In a saucepan, combine the pineapple juice with the remaining 1 1/2 cups sugar. Stir and cook over medium heat for 15 minutes. Remove from the heat and cool. Mix the sugar-pineapple syrup together with the eggs. Then strain and pour into the mold. Set the mold in a larger pan and pour about 1 inch of hot water around the mold. Bake in a preheated 350°F oven for 45 minutes. Remove the mold from its water bath and cool at room temperature before serving.

Yield: 6 to 8 servings

Pineapple Mousse

Mousse a l'Ananas is one of the truly great-tasting desserts from the French Caribbean. Everyone should try this since the ingredients are readily available.

For a more full-bodied mousse, increase the cornstarch to $1/2$ cup. The custard sauce can be made from 1 cup heavy cream instead of light cream.

2 cups fresh or bottled unsweetened pineapple juice
1 cup sugar
1/4 cup cornstarch
Pinch salt
6 egg whites

In a saucepan, combine about two-thirds of the pineapple juice with the sugar. Mix the remaining one-third of the pineapple juice with the cornstarch. Stir until smooth, then add to the saucepan. Cook over medium heat for about 5 minutes, stirring constantly. Cool and set aside.

In a bowl, add a pinch of salt to the egg whites and beat until stiff. Fold into the pineapple mixture, leaving no traces of white. Pour into a serving bowl and chill for about 3 hours. Serve with the Pineapple Custard Sauce.

PINEAPPLE CUSTARD SAUCE

6 egg yolks
1/4 cup sugar
Pinch salt
1 cup light cream, scalded
1 cup chopped fresh pineapple
1 teaspoon vanilla extract

In a bowl, beat the egg yolks with the sugar and salt until a pale yellow. Whisk in the scalded cream. Place the mixture in the top of a double boiler and cook over hot water, stirring constantly, until the mixture is thick. Remove from the heat and stir until cool. Strain and add the chopped pineapple and vanilla. Stir and chill. Spoon the sauce over each individual serving of mousse.

Yield: 6 to 8 servings

Mango Cream Mold

1 cup light cream
1 cup mango puree
1/2 cup sugar
1 tablespoon lime juice
1 tablespoon unflavored
    gelatin
1 tablespoon warm water
Mango slices
Whipped cream

Combine the cream and mango puree, then stir in the sugar and lime juice. Dissolve the gelatin in the warm water and add to the mango mixture. Blend well and beat until creamy.

Pour into an 8-inch ring mold and chill until set, about 3 hours. Unmold onto a serving platter and fill the center with mango slices or any other fresh fruit and whipped cream.

Yield: 4 to 6 servings

Mango Mousse

4 cups canned or fresh mango
    puree
1/4 cup lime juice
1/2 cup sugar
1 tablespoon unflavored
    gelatin
1/4 cup hot water
2 egg whites
1/4 cup heavy cream

Blend the mango puree with the lime juice, stir in the sugar, and mix well. Dissolve the gelatin in the hot water and let stand until cooled. Then stir into the mango puree.

Beat the egg whites until frothy. Whip the cream and fold into the egg whites, then fold into the puree, gently but thoroughly. Pour into a serving bowl and refrigerate until set, about 3 hours.

Yield: 6 servings

Baked Banana Custard Delight

This version of baked banana is mine, but it is derived from a recipe found on most of the islands. It is excellent with ice cream.

5 ripe bananas, peeled and
   mashed
6 tablespoons sugar
1/2 teaspoon freshly grated
   nutmeg
1 tablespoon lime juice
1/2 cup unseasoned dried
   bread crumbs
3 eggs, beaten
1/2 teaspoon vanilla extract
2 cups milk, scalded

Combine the mashed bananas with 3 tablespoons of the sugar, the nutmeg, and lime juice, mixing to make a paste. Spoon into a buttered 2 1/2-quart baking dish and sprinkle the bread crumbs on top.

Combine the eggs with the remaining 3 tablespoons sugar and the vanilla. Then add to scalded milk. Mix well and gently pour on top of the bread crumbs. Bake in a preheated 350°F oven until the top is golden, about 45 minutes. Serve warm.

Yield: 6 to 8 servings

Coconut Custard

In the Spanish-speaking islands, a dish called *Tembleque* is quite similar, but it is made with coconut milk and cornstarch. In this deliciously sweet recipe from Guadeloupe, the grated coconut meat adds extra flavor.

1 cup sugar
1 cup water
3 cups freshly grated coconut
1 (14-ounce) can sweetened
   condensed milk
4 eggs, lightly beaten
2 tablespoons dark rum
1 teaspoon vanilla extract
1/2 teaspoon cinnamon

Caramelize the sugar by combining it with 1/2 cup water in a saucepan. Stir over low heat until the sugar dissolves. Bring to a boil without burning. The mixture will darken in color. Remove from the heat and stir in the remaining 1/2 cup water. Pour into a lightly buttered 9-inch pie pan or mold and set aside.

In a mixing bowl, combine the coconut, condensed milk, eggs, rum, and vanilla. Mix well. Pour into the prepared pan and set in a larger baking pan with an inch of hot water poured around. Bake in a preheated 325°F oven for 45 minutes. Cool, sprinkle with cinnamon, and serve.

Yield: 6 to 8 servings

Ginger Mousse

Crystallized ginger can be as fiery hot as pepper, so taste yours before measuring and reduce the amount used if desired. Use a food processor or mortar and pestle to grind the ginger. This dessert is found throughout the Caribbean.

1 tablespoon unflavored
   gelatin
1/3 cup water
2 (10-ounce) cans evaporated
   milk, scalded
4 eggs, separated
1/4 cup sugar
1/2 cup light rum
About 1 cup finely ground
   crystallized ginger

Combine the gelatin and water in a bowl and stir well to dissolve the gelatin. Stir in the scalded milk and blend well. Beat the egg yolks with the sugar until a pale yellow. Combine with the milk mixture and stir well. Pour into the top of a double boiler and cook, stirring constantly, until the custard coats the spoon. Remove from heat and cool.

Beat the egg whites until stiff. Add the rum and ginger to the custard and mix well. Fold in the egg whites thoroughly, then pour into a 1 1/2-quart serving dish and refrigerate until set. To serve, spoon into individual dessert bowls.

Yield: 6 servings

Banana Pudding with Hot Rum Sauce

4 medium-size ripe bananas,
  peeled and cut into small
  diagonal slices
$1/4$ cup freshly squeezed lime
  juice
$1/4$ cup sugar
6 slices white bread, cubed
$1/4$ cup butter, at room temperature
1 tablespoon vanilla extract
$1/4$ cup dark rum
1 cup light cream
2 eggs
$1/4$ teaspoon freshly grated
  nutmeg

Combine the bananas, lime juice, and sugar in a bowl and mix. Add the bread, butter, vanilla, rum, and cream and mix well. Beat the eggs well and add the nutmeg. Stir into the banana mixture.

Butter a $2^{1}/2$-quart baking dish and pour in the mixture. Set the dish in a larger baking pan and pour an inch of hot water around the dish. Cover the pudding with aluminum foil and bake in a preheated 350°F oven for $1^{1}/4$ hours, or until a tester comes out clean. Remove the baking dish from the water and cool. Invert the pudding onto a serving dish, cover, and refrigerate for at least 2 hours.

HOT RUM SAUCE

$1/2$ cup sugar
$1/2$ cup water
$1/2$ cup rum

To make the sauce, combine the sugar, water, and rum in a saucepan and bring to a boil, stirring constantly. Pour liberally over the chilled pudding and serve.

Yield: 6 to 8 servings

Bread Pudding with Brandy Sauce

One of my favorites, this delightful dessert comes from Puerto Rico. If you have any stale bread on hand you will not want to miss the opportunity to try this recipe.

1 pound day-old white sandwich bread or rolls, crusts removed

4 cups milk

1 cup homemade coconut cream (page 150) or 1 (8-ounce) can commercial coconut cream (Coco Lopez brand is recommended)

5 eggs, slightly beaten

1/2 teaspoon salt

1/4 cup sugar

1/2 teaspoon ground cinnamon

1/4 cup crushed almonds

1/2 cup raisins

1/4 cup butter, melted

Break the bread into small pieces, place in a bowl, and pour the milk over. Soak for 10 minutes. Mash bread thoroughly, then add all the other ingredients, mixing well. Pour the pudding into a well-greased 2^1/2-quart casserole and set the casserole in a larger pan. Pour about 1 inch of hot water into the larger pan. Bake in a preheated 350°F oven for 1^1/2 hours. Cool, pour Brandy Sauce over the entire pudding, and serve.

BRANDY SAUCE

1/2 cup butter, at room temperature

3/4 cup sugar

2 tablespoons brandy

1/4 cup milk

2 eggs, separated

Cream together the butter and sugar. Add the brandy, milk, and egg yolks. Mix well. Pour into a double boiler and cook over hot water until slightly thick, stirring with a wooden spoon to prevent lumps. Cool.

Beat the egg whites until frothy, then fold into the brandy mixture. Stir and pour the sauce over the pudding.

Yield: 6 to 8 servings

Breadfruit Pudding

This recipe is from Martinique. A tablespoon of native *rhum* is sometimes poured over the pudding while it cools. Fresh breadfruit is available in Caribbean markets. The already cooked fruit is also available in cans.

1 pound breadfruit, peeled,
    cooked, and mashed
1/2 cup sugar
1/4 cup butter, melted
1 tablespoon cornstarch
1 teaspoon grated lemon peel
2 cups light cream
2 eggs, lightly beaten
1 teaspoon vanilla extract
2 tablespoons dark rum

Combine all the ingredients in a bowl and beat until smooth. Pour the batter into a well-buttered baking dish and bake in a preheated 350°F oven for about 1³/4 hours, or until a tester comes out clean. Serve warm with a cream sauce, a rum sauce, or ice cream.

NOTE: *To prepare fresh breadfruit, peel and slice the fruit in half, remove the core, cube, and cook as you would potatoes, boiling for 15 to 20 minutes.*

Yield: 6 to 8 servings

Sweet Potato Pudding

So filling is this pudding, a slice can be eaten on the run as a snack, or suffice as lunch for a child.

2 pounds sweet potatoes,
    peeled and finely grated
1 cup brown sugar
3 cups coconut milk
    (page 149)
1 teaspoon ground cinnamon
1 tablespoon butter
1 teaspoon ground ginger
1 teaspoon vanilla extract
1/4 teaspoon grated nutmeg
1/4 cup raisins
1/2 to 1 cup water (optional)

Combine the finely grated potatoes with the sugar, coconut milk, cinnamon, butter, ginger, vanilla, nutmeg, and raisins in a bowl and mix thoroughly. Up to 1 cup of water can be added to the mixture if it is too thick and a softer consistency is desired. Pour the batter into a greased 2¹/2-quart baking pan and bake in a preheated 350°F oven for 1¹/2 hours. Cool to room temperature, slice, and serve. This is especially good with a dab of whipped cream or a scoop of ice cream on top.

Yield: 10 to 12 servings

Arrowroot Custard

Arrowroot, a white starchy powder from a rhizome, is very popular on the islands of the eastern Caribbean. It is used as a thickener for sauces and gravies and in baking and dessert recipes. Arrowroot custard makes a tasty and smooth substitute for ice cream or whipped cream.

2 tablespoons arrowroot
   powder
1 (14-ounce) can evaporated
   milk
1/4 cup sugar
3 eggs, well beaten
1 teaspoon vanilla extract

Combine the arrowroot powder and evaporated milk in a saucepan and cook over low heat for 5 minutes. Stir in the sugar and continue to cook until the mixture is thick and the sugar has dissolved. Stir in the eggs. Reduce the heat and stir for another 5 minutes. Cool, add the vanilla, then chill.

Yield: 2 1/2 cups

Banana Cake

1 1/2 cups all-purpose flour
1 teaspoon baking soda
1 teaspoon baking powder
3 ripe bananas, mashed
1/4 cup butter, at room
   temperature
Pinch salt
2 tablespoons milk
1 egg, beaten
1 cup white sugar
1 teaspoon vanilla extract
1/2 cup brown sugar
1 tablespoon lime juice
1 tablespoon butter

Sift together the flour, baking soda, and baking powder in a bowl. Cream together the bananas, 1/4 cup butter, salt, milk, egg, white sugar, and vanilla until smooth. Pour the batter into a well-buttered 9-inch loaf pan and bake in a preheated 350°F oven for 45 minutes. Cool in the pan for 10 minutes, then remove from the pan and set on a serving plate.

    While the cake is still warm, combine the brown sugar, lime juice, and 1 tablespoon butter in a saucepan. Heat, stirring constantly, until the sugar dissolves. Pour over the warm cake and serve.

Yield: 6 servings

Baked Bananas

This recipe is from the island of St. Lucia, where it is known as *Banane Boulangers.* Sometimes the bananas are peeled and left whole.

6 large ripe bananas, peeled and sliced lengthwise
1 teaspoon freshly grated nutmeg
1/2 cup white rum
1 cup sugar
1/2 cup water
1/2 cup butter, melted

Place the banana slices in a well-buttered shallow casserole. Grate the nutmeg on top, and bake in a preheated 400°F oven for 15 minutes, then set aside.

Combine the rum, sugar, water, and butter in a small saucepan over low heat away from an open flame, and stir until the sugar dissolves. Remove from heat and pour over the baked bananas. Serve hot with a spoonful of the rum sauce poured over each serving.

Yield: 6 servings

Lemon Tart

I have also tasted this tart made from the juice of the large yellow-skinned limes that proliferate throughout the Caribbean.

3 eggs, slightly beaten
2/3 cup sugar
Juice and the grated rind of 4 lemons
9-inch partially baked tart shell (page 140)

In a bowl, combine the eggs, sugar, lemon juice, and grated rind. Mix well. Pour into the pastry shell and bake in a preheated 350°F oven for 30 minutes, or until filling is set and golden. Cool and serve at room temperature

NOTE: *Any kind of fruit glaze can be brushed over the top of the finished tart.*

Yield: 8 servings

Mango Tart

This tart is superb when served with a topping of whipped cream or vanilla ice cream.

4 to 5 ripe mangoes, peeled
   and thinly sliced
1 cup sugar
1/2 cup water
1 teaspoon cornstarch
2 egg yolks, beaten
1 teaspoon ground cinnamon
2 tablespoons butter
9-inch unbaked tart shell
   (page 140)

Combine the mango slices, sugar, and water in a saucepan and cook over medium heat for 15 minutes, stirring constantly. Mix the cornstarch with just enough water to form a paste and blend with the egg yolks. Add to the mango mixture and cook for another 5 minutes, or until it becomes thick and smooth. Stir in the cinnamon and butter.

Pour into the tart shell and bake in a preheated 350°F oven for 30 minutes, or until filling is well set and the top is golden brown. Cool and serve at room temperature.

Yield: 8 servings

Tablettes

The recipe for these particular coconut sugar candies comes from St. Lucia, but variations are to be found throughout the Caribbean, especially from street peddlers. In Jamaica, red food coloring is added to form a pattern on the top of the finished candy, which is then called pink-on-top.

2 cups freshly grated coconut
   (brown skin removed)
1 1/2 cups sugar
1/4 cup water
Dash red food coloring
   (optional)

Combine the grated coconut, sugar, and water in a saucepan and place over medium heat. Stir constantly until the mixture thickens and leaves the sides of the saucepan. Mix in the food coloring if desired. Drop by the tablespoonful onto waxed paper and cool. Store at room temperature, tightly covered.

Yield: About 30 candies

Coconut Bread

Although this particular recipe hails from Grenada, similar coconut breads are found throughout the islands. Coconut bread is usually served with jelly or preserves and eaten as a snack.

2 cups freshly grated coconut
1 cup sugar
2 eggs, well beaten
1 cup evaporated milk
1 teaspoon vanilla extract
1/4 teaspoon ground cinnamon
1/4 cup seedless raisins
2 tablespoons butter, melted
3 cups all-purpose flour
1 tablespoon baking powder
Pinch salt

In a large bowl, combine the coconut and sugar. In another bowl, combine the eggs, milk, vanilla, cinnamon, raisins, and butter in a bowl. Stir this mixture into the grated coconut. Sift in the flour, baking powder, and salt. Combine, mixing until smooth. Pour the batter into 2 greased 9-inch loaf pans, and bake in a preheated 350°F oven for 1 hour, or until a tester comes out clean. Set the pans on wire racks to cool for 10 minutes. Remove the breads from the pans and continue cooling on the wire racks.

Yield: 2 loaves

Banana Bread

The multi-purpose banana strikes again! This is an old recipe that is found in every Caribbean village and has as many variations as there are cooks. Definitely a favorite with children.

1/2 pound butter
1 cup sugar
1 egg
3 large ripe bananas, mashed
2 cups all-purpose flour
1 tablespoon baking powder
1/2 cup milk
1/2 teaspoon ground cinnamon
1/2 teaspoon freshly grated
    nutmeg
Pinch salt
1 teaspoon vanilla extract
1/4 cup raisins

Cream together the butter and sugar. Add the egg and beat thoroughly. Add the bananas and beat well. Sift the flour and baking powder into the mixture. Then add the milk, cinnamon, nutmeg, salt, and vanilla. Blend, then add the raisins and mix well. Pour the batter into a buttered 9-inch loaf pan.

Bake in a preheated 350°F oven for 1 hour, or until a tester comes out clean. Place the pan on a wire rack to cool for 10 minutes. Then remove the bread from the pan and continue cooling on the wire rack. Serve as a snack or as a dessert.

Yield: 1 loaf

Drink Measures

1 dash	=	$1/8$ teaspoon
1 teaspoon	=	$1/8$ ounce
1 tablespoon	=	3 teaspoons
1 pony	=	1 ounce
1 jigger	=	$1^1/2$ ounces
1 wine glass	=	4 ounces or $1/2$ cup
1 split	=	6 ounces or $3/4$ cup
1 cup	=	8 ounces

BEVERAGES AND PARTY DRINKS

No Caribbean meal is truly complete without the accompaniment of one of the region's tasty beverages—spicy or spiked. Even though some of these drinks are readily available in the supermarket, there is something special about preparing one's own mix. Furthermore, many of the ingredients that add that special something are not combined in the commercially prepared beverages. For example, the drink sorrel is available commercially bottled, but it is made without rum, which is a must for that special taste.

Rum is a popular ingredient in a number of recipes. After all, it was seventeenth-century Caribbean that gave birth to the "Rumbullion, alias Kill-Divil . . . a hot, hellish and terrible liquor." Later, Virginian gentlemen began their days with the morning's bombo, or toddy, a smooth blend of rum, sugar, water, and nutmeg.

Rum makes a pleasant addition to food and drink, and some family favorites like egg nog would not be the same without it. The amount of rum used can be increased or decreased to suit the imbiber's fancy; so do not hesitate, go mix your favorite grog.

If you use commercially prepared ingredients in any of the recipes, check to see whether or not they contain sugar, if they are concentrates, or if they are artificially flavored. Read the labels carefully, then adjust your recipes accordingly.

Unless otherwise specified, the fruit juices used can be fresh or bottled.

Calypso Punch

2 cups orange juice
1¹/2 cups (12 ounces)
    sweetened pineapple juice
¹/4 cup lime or lemon juice
2 cups water
¹/4 teaspoon freshly grated
    nutmeg
¹/4 cup honey
6 cloves
2 (12-ounce) cans ginger ale

In a large bowl, mix together all the ingredients, except the ginger ale. Chill, then strain and remove cloves. Add the ginger ale when you are ready to serve. Serve over cracked ice.

Yield: About 9 cups

Tropical Punch

1 cup orange juice
1 cup sweetened pineapple
    juice
1 cup grapefruit juice
1 (12-ounce) can ginger ale

Mix together all the ingredients, except the ginger ale. Chill. Add the ginger ale when you are ready to serve. Serve over shaved ice.

Yield: 4¹/2 cups

Papaya Drink

Franchises pushing the healthful drink, which is also called Papaw and Paw-paw, abound in the U.S. However, for those cooks with time and a sweet tooth, this is a delicious homemade drink.

4 cups ripe papaya
4 cups water
1 (14-ounce) can sweetened
    condensed milk
¹/4 teaspoon Angostura bitters

Puree the papaya in a blender or food processor. Strain and combine with the water and milk. Mix well, add the Angostura, and serve over crushed ice.

Yield: About 2¹/2 quarts

Guava Drink

Guava, a native Caribbean fruit, is now grown in Florida and California. Guavas are rich in vitamin C and minerals.

6 ripe guavas
1 cup boiling water
1 teaspoon lime or lemon
  juice
3 tablespoons sugar

Peel the guavas and cut each in half, then remove the seeds. Pour the boiling water over the skins and steep for 1 hour. Puree the guava halves in a blender or food processor, then combine with the water from the skins, and pass the mixture through a sieve. Add the lime or lemon juice and sugar. Mix thoroughly and serve in tall glasses over cracked ice

Yield: 2 servings

Papaya and Mango Drink

1¹/2 cups (12 ounces) canned
  mango nectar
1¹/2 cups (12 ounces) canned
  papaya nectar
1 cup freshly squeezed orange
  juice
1 teaspoon grated orange peel
2 tablespoons lime or lemon
  juice
3 cups water
Sugar to taste

Combine all the ingredients in an electric blender and blend well. Strain, chill, and serve over cracked ice.

Yield: About 7 cups

Refresco de Coco y Piña

This Coconut and Pineapple Drink is a refreshing combination from the Dominican Republic, where a dash of rum is sometimes added for emphasis.

2 cups coconut milk
   (page 149)
2¹/2 cups chopped fresh or
   canned pineapple
2 tablespoons fine granulated
   sugar
Dash almond extract

Combine all the ingredients in an electric blender and puree. Strain, refrigerate, and chill. Serve in frosted glasses.

Yield: 4 cups

Carrot Drink

A popular Caribbean drink, the canned and watered-down version found in shops lack the milk and cannot compare to your own.

6 large carrots
1 cup water
1 teaspoon lime or lemon juice
1 cup sugar
2 cups milk

Grate the carrots in an electric juicer, blender, or food processor. Then mix with water and press through a sieve. Strain and add the lime or lemon juice to the carrot and water mixture. Add the sugar and milk. Mix well, chill, and serve.

Yield: 4 servings

Tamarind Drink

Called Tamarinade in Jamaica, a version is also available canned, but without the fizziness the baking soda adds. Tamarind pulp is also used in some pepper condiments and curries.

1 pound tamarind pulp
1 quart water
1 teaspoon ground ginger
3 cups brown sugar
2 teaspoons baking soda

Soak the tamarind in 1 quart of water overnight. Add the ginger and allow the mixture to sit for 1 hour. Strain and add the sugar. Refrigerate and chill. Add the baking soda just before serving and stir.

Yield: About 5 cups

Bacardi Cocktail

1 1/2 ounces Bacardi light rum
1 ounce lime or lemon juice
1 teaspoon grenadine
Cracked ice (2 ice cubes)

Combine the rum, lime or lemon juice, and grenadine. Shake with the cracked ice, then strain into a cocktail glass, and serve.

Yield: 1 serving

Between the Sheets

1 1/2 ounces dark or light rum
1/2 ounce Triple Sec
1/2 ounce brandy
1 ounce lemon juice
Cracked ice (2 ice cubes)

Combine the rum, Triple Sec, brandy, and lemon juice. Shake well with the cracked ice and strain into a cocktail glass.

Yield: 1 serving

Blue Mountain Cocktail

This drink was named after Jamaica's highest mountain range, famous for the coffee grown there. It is also claimed by the Blue Mountain Inn, one of the island's premiere restaurants. The distinguishing flavor in the Blue Mountain Cocktail comes from the coffee liqueur, Tia Maria, also a native Jamaican.

$1^1/2$ ounces light Jamaican
   rum
$3/4$ ounce vodka
$3/4$ ounce Tia Maria
2 ounces orange juice
1 ounce lime juice
3 ice cubes

Combine the rum, vodka, Tia Maria, orange juice, and the lime juice. Shake well with the ice cubes. Pour into an old-fashioned glass and serve.

Yield: 1 serving

Bossanova

1 ounce dark or light rum
$1/4$ ounce Galliano
$1/4$ ounce apricot brandy
2 ounces apple juice
$1/4$ ounce lemon juice
Crushed ice (2 cubes)
Orange slice
Cherry

Combine the rum, Galliano, brandy, apple juice, and lemon juice. Shake well with the crushed ice and strain into a collins glass. Garnish with the orange slice and a cherry.

Yield: 1 serving

Cuba Libre

1 1/2 ounces light rum
3 ounces cola
Dash lime juice
Ice cubes
Lime wedge

Mix the rum, cola, and lime juice in a tall glass filled with ice cubes. Stir well and garnish with a lime wedge.

Yield: 1 serving

El Presidente

1 1/2 ounces light rum
3/4 ounce dry vermouth
Dash Angostura bitters
Cracked ice (2 ice cubes)

Combine the rum, vermouth, and Angostura. Shake with the cracked ice. Strain into a cocktail glass and serve.

Yield: 1 serving

Petit Punch

An aperitif from the French islands, Martinique and Guadeloupe, this "little" rum punch is usually drunk neat—without ice.

1½ ounces white rum
1 tablespoon sugar syrup
¼ ounce lime juice
Water

Combine all the ingredients in a mixing glass and mix well. Serve in a cocktail glass.

NOTE: *To make a sugar syrup, combine equal amounts of water and sugar in a saucepan and heat, stirring constantly, until the sugar dissolves. Store, covered, in the refrigerator; it will keep for several months.*

Yield: 1 serving

Jamaica Planter's Punch

1 tablespoon strawberry-
    flavored syrup or 2 table-
    spoons grenadine
2 tablespoons fine granulated
    sugar
1 teaspoon lime or lemon
    juice
4 ounces dark or light
    Jamaican rum
Shaved ice
Orange slice
Diced fresh or canned
    pineapple
Mint sprigs

Combine the syrup or grenadine, sugar, lime or lemon juice, and rum. Shake well. Serve over shaved ice in a collins glass. Garnish with sliced orange, diced pineapple, and mint.

Yield: 1 serving

Rum Collins

1½ ounces dark rum
1 ounce lemon juice
1 teaspoon fine granulated
    sugar
Cracked ice (3 ice cubes)
Club soda
Lime wedge
Cherry

Shake the rum, lemon juice, and sugar with cracked ice. Pour into a collins glass and fill with club soda. Garnish with a lime wedge and a cherry and serve with a straw.

Yield: 1 serving

Rum Rickey

1½ ounces dark or light rum
1 ounce lime juice
3 ice cubes
Club soda
Lime wedge

Mix the rum and lime juice in a collins glass with the ice and fill with club soda. Stir and garnish with a lime wedge.

Yield: 1 serving

Rum Sour

1¹/2 ounces dark or light rum
1 ounce lemon juice
1 egg white, lightly beaten
¹/2 teaspoon fine granulated
　sugar
Cracked ice (2 ice cubes)
Orange slice
Cherry

Shake the rum, lemon juice, egg white, and sugar with the cracked ice. Then strain into a cocktail glass. Garnish with an orange slice and a cherry.

Yield: 1 serving

Rum Swizzle

³/4 ounce lime juice
2 ounces club soda
Ice cubes
2 ounces dark or light rum
2 dashes Angostura bitters

Mix the lime juice and 1 ounce of the club soda in a collins glass filled with ice. Stir with a swizzle stick, then add the rum and Angostura. Fill with the rest of the club soda. Stir and serve.

Yield: 1 serving

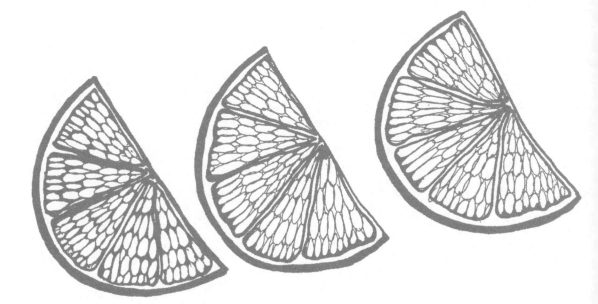

Scorpion

4 tablespoons fine granulated
    sugar
1/4 cup water
1/4 cup lime juice
4 dashes Angostura
4 ounces dark or light rum

Combine the sugar and water in a small pot and cook until the mixture darkens. Cool, then add the lime juice and Angostura. Mix, add the rum and blend well. Strain over ice cubes in a cocktail glass.

Yield: 2 servings

Steel Band

1 1/2 ounces gold rum
4 ounces orange juice
Cracked ice (2 ice cubes)
5 dashes Angostura bitters
Lime or lemon peel

Pour the rum and orange juice over cracked ice in a prechilled glass. Add the Angostura, stir, garnish with lime or lemon peel, and serve.

Yield: 1 serving

Trinidad Cocktail

2 ounces Trinidad rum
1 ounce lime juice
4 dashes Angostura bitters
Cracked ice (2 ice cubes)
Lime or lemon peel

Shake the rum, lime juice, and Angostura with the cracked ice and strain into a glass. Garnish with lime or lemon peel.

Yield: 1 serving

Trinidad Punch

1/4 cup finely cracked ice
4 dashes Angostura bitters
1 ounce lime or lemon juice
1 tablespoon fine granulated
   sugar
3 ounces Trinidad rum
Twist of lime or lemon peel

Place the ice in a mixing glass. Add the Angostura, lime or lemon juice, sugar, and rum. Mix well, then strain into a glass, garnish with lime or lemon peel, and serve.

Yield: 2 servings

Yellow Bird

The yellow-colored parakeet, found in great numbers throughout the Caribbean, was immortalized in a Harry Belafonte version of a Haitian folk song, *"Tits Oiseau"* ("Yellow bird up high in banana tree"). Traditionally sun by balladeers at hotels and teary-eyed tourists on their departure from the beautiful island-paradise, the song has been adopted by most Caribbean havens. The origins of this drink are unknown, but visitors request it frequently.

1 ounce dark or light rum
1/2 ounce Galliano
1/2 ounce Triple Sec
1 ounce lemon juice
2 ice cubes

Blend all the ingredients with the ice and strain into a cocktail glass.

Yield: 1 serving

Daiquiri

1¹/2 ounces light rum
1 ounce lime juice
1 teaspoon fine granulated
    sugar
Cracked ice (2 ice cubes)

Combine the rum, lime juice, and sugar and shake with the cracked ice. Strain into a cocktail glass and serve.

Yield: 1 serving

Frozen Daiquiri

1¹/2 ounces light rum
1 ounce lime juice
1 teaspoon fine granulated
    sugar
Crushed ice

Mix the rum, lime juice, and sugar with the crushed ice and blend for 30 seconds. Pour into a champagne glass and serve with 2 short straws.

Yield: 1 serving

Banana Daiquiri

1¹/2 ounces light rum
1 tablespoon Triple Sec
¹/2 ripe banana, peeled
¹/2 ounce lime juice
1 cup crushed ice

Combine all the ingredients in an electric blender and puree for 30 seconds. Serve in a cocktail glass.

Yield: 1 serving

Banshee

¹/2 ounce crème de banana
¹/2 ounce crème de cacao
¹/2 ounce heavy cream
Cracked ice (2 ice cubes)

Combine the liqueurs and cream. Shake with the crushed ice, strain into a cocktail glass, and serve.

Yield: 1 serving

Bahama Mama

¹/2 ounce light rum
2 ounces apple juice
¹/2 ounce cream of coconut
1 ounce orange juice
Dash Triple Sec
Dash grenadine

Combine the rum, apple juice, cream of coconut, orange juice, Triple Sec, and grenadine in an electric blender. Process for about 30 seconds, then strain over crushed ice in a collins glass, and serve.

Yield: 1 serving

Punch au Lait de Coco

Coconut Milk Punch is a smooth, delicious drink from Martinique. The local *rhum blanc*—white rum—adds to this tasty drink.

3 ounces light rum
1 cup coconut milk (page 149)
2 tablespoons sugar syrup
*   (see note on page 124)*
1/4 teaspoon vanilla extract
crushed ice
Pinch freshly ground nutmeg

Combine the rum, coconut milk, sugar syrup, and vanilla in a mixing glass and shake well. Strain over crushed ice in a collins glass and sprinkle with freshly ground nutmeg.

Yield: 2 servings

Piña Colada

1¹/₂ ounces rum
1 ounce coconut milk
*   (page 149)*
2 ounces unsweetened
*   pineapple juice or ¹/₄ cup*
*   fresh pineapple chunks*
1 ounce lime juice
Cracked ice (2 ice cubes)
Pineapple spears

Combine the rum, coconut milk, pineapple juice, and lime juice in a blender with the cracked ice. Blend for about 30 seconds. Strain into a collins glass filled with shaved ice. Garnish with pineapple spears and serve with a straw.

Yield: 1 serving

Rum and Coconut Water

Tradition says this drink is healthful!

1 or more coconuts
2 ounces white rum

Puncture the "eyes" (black spots on the top of coconut). Pour the water from the nut into a glass. (Make sure the coconut milk is not rancid by smelling it.) Strain and serve with rum over ice cubes.

Yield: 1 serving

Cold Rum Toddy

1 teaspoon fine granulated
    sugar
Splash club soda
1¹/2 ounces dark rum
Twist lemon peel

Dissolve the sugar in the club soda in an old-fashioned glass. Add 1 ice cube and the rum. Garnish with a twist of lemon peel. Stir and serve.

Yield: 1 serving

Hot Rum Toddy

1 teaspoon fine granulated
　sugar
¹/2 cup boiling water
1¹/2 ounces dark rum
Pinch freshly ground nutmeg

Dissolve the sugar in the boiling water in a small pot. Transfer to an old-fashioned glass and add the rum, stirring. Sprinkle nutmeg over the top and serve.

Yield: 1 serving

Hot Buttered Rum

3 ounces dark rum
1 teaspoon fine granulated
　sugar
1 teaspoon butter
2 dashes Angostura bitters
Boiling water
Whole cloves or ground
　nutmeg

Mix the rum, sugar, butter, and Angostura in a mug. Fill with boiling water and stir well. Sprinkle with whole cloves or ground nutmeg and serve.

Yield: 1 serving

Egg Nog Tropicale

This is a favorite concoction of mine—great for Sunday mornings. The rum is generous in this recipe and can be toned down if you prefer.

6 eggs, separated
2 cups milk
1/2 cup fine granulated sugar
2 cups dark rum
1/4 teaspoon lime or lemon
    juice
1 teaspoon vanilla extract
1/2 teaspoon freshly grated
    nutmeg

Beat the egg whites until stiff and set aside. Beat the egg yolks lightly, then beat in the milk and sugar. Fold in the egg whites, then mix in the rum, lime or lemon juice, and vanilla. Cover and chill. Stir well, sprinkle nutmeg on top, and serve in 4-ounce punch glasses or cups.

Yield: 8 servings

Punch à Créme

An Eastern Caribbean Christmastime favorite, this drink is akin to egg nog.

6 eggs
1 lime peel, coarsely chopped
1 (7-ounce) can evaporated
    milk
1 (10-ounce) can sweetened
    condensed milk
1/4 cup dark rum
1 teaspoon Angostura bitters

Beat the eggs with the lime peel. Remove and discard the peel. In the top half of a double boiler, combine the beaten eggs with the milk, stir well, and heat over boiling water until the mixture is thick and smooth. Remove from the heat and cool. Stir in the rum and bitters, bottle, and chill. Shake well before serving over cracked ice.

Yield: 2$^{1}/_{2}$ cups

Jamaica Rum Punch

If strawberry-flavored syrup is unavailable, grenadine can be substituted, but increase the honey to 1 cup.

4 cups water
1 cup lime or lemon juice
1/2 cup honey
6 cloves or allspice berries
2 cups strawberry-flavored
 syrup
1 teaspoon freshly grated
 nutmeg
2 cups Jamaican white rum

Mix all ingredients together in a punch bowl, and let the mixture settle for 1 hour before removing the cloves or allspice. Stir and serve over ice cubes in old-fashioned glasses.

Yield: 10 to 12 servings

Mango Punch

1 dozen ripe mangoes or
 1 (19-ounce) can mango
 nectar
4 cups water
3 ounces dark or light rum
1 cup fine granulated sugar

Wash and peel the mangoes, then remove the pulp from the seeds. Puree the mango pulp in a blender or food processor. Then combine the mango puree (or canned nectar if used) with the water in a saucepan and bring to a rolling boil. Simmer for 15 minutes, then cool. Add the rum and sugar. Mix well, strain, and serve chilled.

Yield: 8 to 10 servings

Sorrel Drink

No matter what time of year sorrel shoots are planted, they always bloom in late November or early December. Even if the shoots are planted in January, the red flower (which generally takes 6 months to appear) blooms only shortly before the Christmas season. Fresh sorrel is imported in early December and can be found in markets or greengrocers that carry Caribbean produce. Packaged dried sorrel is sold at Caribbean food counters year-round.

3 dozen fresh sorrel sepals or
  1 (2-ounce) packet dried
3 fingers fresh ginger, peeled
  (4 ounces)
3 to 4 limes or lemons,
  halved
2 quarts boiling water
2¼ cups brown sugar
½ cup Jamaica white rum

If the sorrel is fresh, first strip off the red sepals and discard the buds. Then combine the sepals or the dried sorrel with the ginger in a large bowl. Pour the boiling water over the sorrel and ginger. Squeeze the limes or lemons and add the juice and peels to the bowl. Steep for at least a day, then strain out the solids. Sweeten with the brown sugar and add the rum. Chill and serve over cracked ice.

NOTE: *The process can be repeated with the solid residues of the first batch, though the brew will taste weaker.*

Yield: 2½ quarts

Pineapple Liqueur

4 cups diced fresh pineapple
2 cups lime or lemon juice
4 cups brown sugar
Cloves
2 cups white rum

Combine the pineapple, lime or lemon juice, sugar, and cloves. Place the mixture in a cheesecloth set over a bowl, and leave overnight to drain. The next day, add the rum to the drained liquid and allow to sit for 2 hours. Serve as a liqueur.

Yield: Approximately 20 to 26 servings

BASIC RECIPES

Sofrito

Sofrito is a basic flavoring mixture added to many Puerto Rican and Spanish dishes, including pilaffs, stews, rice, and beans.

2 ounces salt pork, diced
2 tablespoons lard with
  annatto or saffron
1 small onion, chopped
1 garlic clove, crushed
1 (6-ounce) can tomato sauce
1 green pepper, seeded and
  finely chopped
2 ounces ham, diced
6 olives
1 teaspoon capers

Sauté the salt pork in a skillet until all the fat is released. Add the lard, onion, and garlic and stir until the onion is translucent. Reduce the heat and add the tomato sauce, green pepper, ham, olives, and capers. Simmer for 15 minutes, stirring occasionally. Cool, bottle, and refrigerate until needed.

Yield: 1 cup

Colombo

A powder brought to the French Caribbean by East Indians in the mid-nineteenth century, colombo is a homemade curry seasoning still made and used by many cooks.

2 small hot red peppers
2 teaspoons ground coriander
2 teaspoons dry mustard
4 garlic cloves, crushed
1/4 teaspoon tumeric
Water (optional)

Combine all the ingredients and pulverize with a pestle. Mix until a paste forms, adding a little water to moisten. This makes enough curry flavoring for chicken, goat, pork, lamb, beef, or fish.

Yield: Curry flavoring to serve 8

Cassareep

The thick and syrup residue of the raw cassava, cassareep is an ancient Amerindian food enhancer and preservative. This traditional specialty is used in one of Guyana's national dishes, Pepperpot. Cassareep is sometimes laced with hot peppers, but since pepper is usually added to dishes cassareep graces, the faint-hearted are advised to abstain from adding the fiery devil to this recipe.

4 pounds sweet cassava (yuca,
    yucca, or manioc), peeled
    and chunked
1 cup water
1/4 teaspoon ground cloves
1/2 teaspoon ground cinnamon
1/2 teaspoon salt
4 teaspoons brown sugar

With a hand grater or in an electric blender or food processor, grate the cassava. Then add the water and mix well. Squeeze the mixture through a sieve or a dampened cheesecloth, extracting and retaining all the liquid in a saucepan and discarding the solids. Add the cloves, cinnamon, salt, and sugar, and bring to a boil. Reduce the heat and simmer, stirring until the liquid becomes thick. Store covered in a refrigerator until you are ready to use it.

Yield: About 1 cup

Patty Pastry

2 cups all-purpose flour
1 teaspoon baking powder
$^1/_2$ teaspoon salt
$^1/_2$ cup vegetable shortening
$^1/_4$ cup cold water

Sift together the flour, baking powder, and salt in a bowl. Rub in the shortening and water without kneading too much as the dough will become too elastic and heavy. Mix until the dough has the consistency of bread crumbs, and roll into a ball. Lightly dust the dough with flour, wrap in plastic film or waxed paper, and refrigerate for at least an hour.

When ready to fill, roll out the dough on a floured board as thinly as possible, about $^1/_8$ inch thick. Cut out circles of dough about 5 inches in diameter. Fill and bake as directed.

Yield: Pastry for 12 patties

Tart Shell

Add the sugar to the dough only if you are baking a dessert pie.

1¹/2 cups all-purpose flour
1 tablespoon sugar (optional)
¹/2 cup chilled butter
2 tablespoons or more cold
    water

Combine the flour and sugar in a bowl. Rub in the butter and mix until flaky, not smooth. Sprinkle water over and lightly mix with your hand. Shape the dough into a ball, wrap, and refrigerate for about 1 hour.

Roll out the pastry on a lightly floured board to form a 12-inch circle and place it in a 9-inch pan. Trim the excess fringe of dough and crimp the edges. Prick the bottom of the dough, and line it with aluminum foil. Weight down the foil with about 1 cup of rice or dried beans to get a perfectly formed shell.

Place the pastry shell in a preheated 400°F oven and bake for 5 minutes. Remove the foil and return the pastry shell to the oven and bake for another 5 minutes, or until the shell begins to turn a light golden color. Remove from the oven to obtain a partially baked shell. For a fully baked shell, reduce the heat to 350°F and bake for 20 to 25 minutes.

Yield: 9-inch tart shell

Roti Dough

Traditionally, rotis are cooked on a flat iron griddle called a *tawa,* but any heavy skillet or griddle can be used. If the rotis are to be filled with any curried meat, poultry, or vegetable and eaten as a finger food, make 12-inch rotis. Place the filling in the center and fold in the edges. When they are to be served as a bread to dip up curries, chutneys, or gravies, prepare 8-inch rotis.

2 cups all-purpose flour
1/4 teaspoon baking soda
1/2 teaspoon salt
Milk to mix
Vegetable oil

Sift together the flour, baking soda, and salt into a bowl. Add enough milk to form a stiff dough. Knead the dough well on a lightly floured board, then form into 4 or more equal-sized balls. Roll out the dough thinly to form 8-inch or 12-inch circles. Then brush on a thin coating of vegetable oil. Roll into balls again, cover, and allow to stand for 15 minutes at room temperature.

Roll out the dough again and flatten to the original dimensions by patting lightly. Heat a cast-iron or heavy-bottomed frying pan so that when tested with a drop of water, it sizzles. Place the rotis, one at a time, in the pan and cook for a minute. Turn, and spread a thin layer of vegetable oil on the surface of each roti, and turn frequently until cooked—when brown flecks appear on the surface. Remove from the frying pan and pound between the palms of the hands until it becomes supple. Keep rotis warm and moist by covering with a towel.

Yield: 4 to 6 servings

Flour Dumplings

There are many varieties of dumplings; the flour dumpling is the most popular in the Caribbean and simplest to make.

1 cup all-purpose flour
1/4 teaspoon salt
Water

Sift the flour and salt into a bowl and slowly add enough cold water to make a stiff dough. (A sticky dough makes a soft, pasty dumpling.) Knead in the bowl or on a lightly floured board until smooth. Shape into small balls that fit in the palm of your hand and flatten in the palm of one hand by using karate-like chops with the other hand.

Immerse into salted boiling water and cook for 15 to 20 minutes. Or add to soups and stews and cook for the same period or longer.

Yield: 6 to 9 dumplings

Johnny cakes

This recipe can be used to make a softer, smoother, and sweeter dumpling than the plain flour dumpling, However, the dough is usually fried to make Johnny Cakes or Journey Cakes. For a thicker consistency, part of the flour is replaced by cornmeal, using 2/3 cup flour and 1/3 cup cornmeal.

1 cup all-purpose flour
1 1/2 teaspoons baking powder
1/4 teaspoon salt
1 tablespoon butter or
  margarine
Water
1/4 cup vegetable oil

Sift the flour, baking powder, and salt into a bowl. Rub in the butter or margarine. Slowly add enough cold water to make a stiff dough. Knead in a bowl or on a lightly floured board until smooth. Shape into small balls that fit in the palm of your hand and flatten in the palm of one hand by using karate-like chops with the other hand.

Heat the vegetable oil in a skillet, then add the dumplings, and fry evenly until golden brown on all sides. Serve warm.

Yield: 6 to 9 dumplings

DIRECTORY OF CARIBBEAN FOOD DISTRIBUTORS

In response to the culinary needs of millions of Caribbean immigrants in the United States, *bodegas,* fresh produce stands, and food stores have sprung up almost overnight in many regions of the country. Some chain supermarkets have also opened specialty sections stocked with Caribbean foods and condiments. The name Goya is synonymous with high-quality packaged Caribbean food products and is distributed nationally. So you should be able to find many of the special Caribbean ingredients at your local supermarket.

The following list comprises businesses that sell fresh and processed Caribbean foods in some areas of the U.S. and Canada. When you can't find an ingredient you need in your local area, try a phone call to the nearest listed business; they may be able to direct you to a retailer in your immediate vicinity. Of course, in cities, such as New York, Washington D.C., Miami, Philadelphia, Detroit, and Hartford—areas of massive Caribbean immigration—ethnic foods are readily available. In New York City, for example, the Bronx Terminal Market and the Brooklyn Terminal Market supply most any Caribbean food product.

California

Goya Foods of California
831 Kohler Street
Los Angeles, CA 90021
(213) 624-2309

La Preferida Meat Market
4471 Whittier Blvd.
Los Angeles, CA 90022
(323) 268-2549

Florida

B & M Bakery & West Indian Grocery
6959 Miramar Parkway
Miramar, FL 33023
 (954) 983-0078

**F A & M West Indian &
American Grocery**
18400 NW 2nd Avenue
Miami, FL 33169
(305) 653-2384

Goya
1900 N.W. 92nd Ave.
Miami, FL 33172
(305) 592-3150

Jamaica Groceries & Spices
9628 S.W. 160th St.
Colonial Shopping Centre
Miami, FL 33157
(305) 252-1197

Kingston-Miami Trading Co.
280 N.E. 2nd St.
Miami, FL 33132
(305) 372-9547

**V & S East & West Indian Food
& Spices**
11654 Quail Roost Drive
Miami, FL 33157
(305) 232-5920

Illinois

Goya Foods, Inc.
1001 Bryn Mawr Avenue
Bensenville, IL 60106
(630) 616-8300

New Jersey

Goya Foods
100 Seaview Dr.
Secaucus, NJ 07094
(201) 348-4900

New York

Bronx Terminal Market
Bronx, NY 10474

Brooklyn Terminal Market
Liberty Avenue
Brooklyn, NY 11207
(718) 444-5700

La Marqueta
106 Broadway
New York, NY 10005
(212) 916-2300

Port Royal Foods, Inc.
95 Froehlich Farm Boulevard
Woodbury, NY 11797
(516) 921-8383

Canada

West Indian Fine Foods
Terrace Brae Plaza
Markham & Lawrence
Scarborough, Ontario M1G 2P5
(416) 431-9353

Solas Market
341 Glendower Circuit
Agincourt
Toronto, Ontario
(416) 291-6567

Toronto Caribbean Corner
171 Baldwin Street
Toronto, Ontario M5T 1L9
(416) 593-0008

GLOSSARY

Ackee *(akee)*—The fruit of an evergreen tree, ackee is found throughout the Caribbean, but it is most abundant in Jamaica, where it is cooked with salt fish to make that country's national dish. Ackee is a triangular fruit with a red coat. When ripe, it splits in three; the yellowish edible portion is the part that is cooked fresh. (Importation of the canned fruit is banned in the U.S., even though some cans are available on occasion. The fruit is allowed through U.S. Customs parboiled, and it is available elsewhere unrestricted.)

Annatto *(achiote, roucou)*—The brick red seeds of the small, flowering annatto tree *(Bixa orellana)* are used mainly as a natural food coloring. You can buy the seeds dried (look for either annatto or achiote seeds) or crushed. In Hispanic stores, it can be found as paste made with pepper, vinegar, salt, and garlic or as a paste made with lard called *manteca de achiote*.

Arrowroot—Extracted from the root of a plant and then ground, arrowroot is a starch that is used to thicken puddings, sauces, and glazes. It is so called because it was used as an antidote to poison caused by arrow wounds. Arrowroot is available in health food stores, specialty food stores, and some supermarkets.

Banana *(banane)*—Both green and ripe bananas are used in Caribbean cooking. They are prepared mashed, whole, creamed, and fried. Small bananas are best for cooking, larger ones are more suitable for eating ripe. Bananas can be used as a substitute for the less widely available plantain. See page 157 for instructions on cooking green bananas.

Breadfruit *(fruit à pain)*—A large green fruit, sometimes 10 to 12 inches in diameter, the breadfruit has a bumpy skin. It is peeled and fried, or cooked like a potato, or roasted in the skin, then peeled. It is served as a starchy vegetable. Breadfruit is available fresh or canned in Spanish and West Indian food stores.

Callaloo *(calalou)*—A green leafy vegetable of the Chinese spinach family, callaloo is widely grown in Jamaica. It is used in soups or served as a vegetable dish. On a menu, Callaloo is either a dish of dasheen leaves, salt pork, and crabs (in Trinidad and Guyana) or a soup (in most other Caribbean countries). The vegetable is available fresh or canned in West Indian food stores.

Cassava *(manioc, yaca, yacca)*—A root vegetable used as an addition to soups and meat dishes. The flour is used in breads and cakes (bammy in Jamaica). Tapioca comes from the cassava. It is widely available in Hispanic grocery stores.

Chili Peppers—Fresh, hot chili peppers of the genus Capsicum are frequently used in Caribbean cooking. The Scotch bonnet is a variety of chili pepper commonly used on the islands, and it is sometimes available in grocery stores that import Caribbean foods. The Scotch bonnet is a medium-sized, round, thick-skinned pepper. It may be red or yellow colored and ranges in size from a quarter to a half-dollar. An acceptable substitute is the commonly available jalapeño. Although much milder in flavor (a quarter to half the heat), the jalapeño is similarly thick skinned; in recipes that call for cooking the whole pepper in the gravy or soup and then removing before serving, the thick skin prevents the pepper from falling apart. If a mildly hot dish is preferred, be sure to seed the chili pepper before chopping and adding to a dish. And always be sure to thoroughly wash your hands, as well as any utensils, after handling chili peppers.

Christophene *(cho-cho, chayote)*—A pale green, pear-shaped squash, the exterior is furrowed and prickly. It is added to soups, stews, and broths, and can be pureed, stuffed, baked, creamed, or steamed. It is available in supermarkets and greengrocers throughout the U.S.

Coconut—Although some packaged coconut products are available in the marketplace, the discerning cook will prefer fresh coconut. If you do decide to use a packaged or canned coconut product, be sure to read the labels carefully, as prepared products are sometimes concentrates, extracts, or dried fruit. Canned coconut cream, which is sweetened and widely available, is used in desserts and drinks. It cannot be used as a substitute for coconut milk.

To open a coconut, place the coconut, eyes down, on a solid surface and crack with a hammer several times. Pry the meat loose from the shell with a blunt knife. If the recipe calls for white meat only (as in shredding), pare off the brown skin with a swivel-bladed peeler or a knife. If you are making milk or cream, it is not necessary to peel the coconut.

Coconut Water—Excellent as a mixer with rum (page 131). Simply pierce the eyes (black spots at one end of the nut) with an ice pick and drain the liquid. Smell before using; sometimes the water is rancid, which does not affect the meat. As long as the meat is white and firm it can be used for shredding and milk or cream extraction, but rancid coconut water should be discarded.

Coconut Milk—Cut the meat into small pieces and grate in a food processor or an electric blender. Moisten with the coconut water or plain hot water, then liquefy until as fine as possible. Pour boiling water on the liquefied coconut and let it stand in a bowl for 30 minutes, then pass through a cheesecloth or sieve to separate the milk from the solids. Discard the solids.

There is no hard and fast rule governing the amount of coconut meat to use per cup of coconut milk. Generally a half a coconut will yield up to 4 cups of a mildly flavored coconut milk, or 2 cups of rich coconut milk. Use as much boiling water as necessary to make the amount of coconut water required in the recipe (ie., if the recipe calls for 2 cups coconut milk, pour 2 cups of boiling water over the liquefied coconut). For very rich milk, squeeze the liquefied coconut through a dampened cheesecloth or press it through a fine sieve, catching the extracted milk in a bowl. Do not pour boiling water over it.

Coconut Cream—Pour rich, undiluted coconut milk into a bowl and allow to stand for at least 4 hours, preferably overnight, in a cool place or in a refrigerator, until a thick cream rises to the top. Skim off and use the cream as needed.

Coconut Oil—Pour rich, undiluted coconut milk into a saucepan and bring the milk to a boil. Reduce the heat and simmer until the water from the milk evaporates. Skim off the cream and you will be left with the oil. Strain and bottle.

Grated Coconut—Peel and discard the brown skin. Then grate the white flesh with a hand-held grater or in an electric blender or food processor. The brown skin can be left on if white coconut is not required.

Shredded Coconut—Peel and discard the brown skin from the flesh and shred as you would carrots.

Conch *(lambi, concha)*—Conch is eaten raw in salads and cooked in soups, stews, and fritters in all the Caribbean islands. It is available fresh or frozen in large fish markets in the United States. If you live in New York City, you will find it at La Marqueta in East Harlem, the country's largest market for fresh and packaged Caribbean foods. Conch probably can be special ordered from your local fish market.

Conch is similar to abalone in that its meat is white and extremely tough. For best results, place the uncooked conch on a chopping board and beat it with a paddle or some heavy object until it is flattened. The conch should be cut into small pieces for easier and quicker cooking.

Dasheen *(tania, taro)*—A tuber with barklike, brown ridged skin. The grey, white, or violet flesh is cut into large cubes for soups or served as a vegetable with meats. The young dasheen shoots and leaves are used much like spinach. It is available in West Indian food markets.

Eddoe *(coco)*—Small, round-bottomed, brown-skinned, and hairy, this vegetable with white or purplish flesh is used in soups and with meats. It is available in West Indian food markets.

Guava—The pink flesh of this tasty plum-size fruit and its green or yellow skin are edible. It is used in beverages, jellies, and sherbets. A ripe guava will give slightly when pressed with the fingers.

Papaya *(paw-paw, papaw)*—A melon-like fruit that is ripe when yellow. The unripe fruit is sometimes cooked like squash. Ripe it is used in condiments, beverages, ice creams, and sherbets, or eaten plain as one would a melon. Papayas are widely available in the produce section of supermarkets and at greengrocers.

Pigeon Peas *(gungo)*—Fresh, they are green colored; dried, they are a mottled brown roundish pea. They are cooked with rice, stewed, and added to soups. Pigeon peas are available in supermarkets packaged dry or canned.

Plantain—A member of the banana family, but larger than the familiar yellow banana. A ripe plantain, which turns black, is not palatable eaten raw; it should be fried, cooked, or baked. Plantains are available in Spanish bodegas and West Indian food shops.

When used in recipes requiring cooked plantains or bananas, you can prepare the green, unripe fruit in one of two ways. Wash the unpeeled fruit, then cut off about 1/4 inch from the pointed ends of the fruit. Slit the skins lengthwise, without damaging the pulp, on two sides of each fruit. Immerse in cold water and boil, covered, for 20 to 30 minutes, or until a sharp knife can penetrate the fruit easily. A pinch of salt can be added to the boiling water for taste, and a dash of vegetable oil can be added for easy removal of the skin. When the fruits are cooked, the skins can be easily removed from the pulp by lifting away with a fork.

When a green banana or a ripe or unripe plantain is to be added to a pot—usually a soup—prepare by washing, then cutting off the ends. Next slit and remove the skin by carefully lifting it away from the pulp with the fingers, or peeling lengthwise with a knife. Then remove the skin and ribbed inner layer without damaging the pulp.

Pumpkin *(calabaza, giromon)*—Not the North American pie and Halloween variety, the Caribbean pumpkin is round or oval in shape, and greenish or yellow and mottled with white in color. Its bright yellow flesh is used in soups or served mashed, or stuffed. Caribbean pumpkins are available in Spanish bodegas and West Indian food shops.

Salt Beef—Salt beef can be found in barrels in specialty food stores that carry Caribbean foods. It is stew beef that has been preserved by salting, just like the more commonly available salted codfish.

Salt Fish *(bacalao, morue)*—Salt fish is the colloquial Caribbean name for dried salted fish, and the name encompasses the several varieties of fish used in island cooking. Although salted cod is the most popular, salted pollock and haddock are good substitutes.

Salted fish is widely available in the United States. Sometimes it will be labeled as *bacalao,* as it is called in Spanish-speaking areas, and some times it is found under the name *morue,* as it is called in the French Caribbean. It can be bought with or without bones. For the best dollar value, buy the salted boneless fillets packaged in 1-pound units.

Before using, soak the fish in cold water for several hours or even overnight to remove the salt. If you don't have time for the overnight soak, a quick way to rid the fish of salt is to place it in a saucepan of cold water and boil. How long to boil depends on the concentration of the salt; different packagers use varying amounts of salt in the preservation process. To determine how long to boil it, you must taste the fish from time to time. Once the fish has been desalted, drain and flake it with a fork.

Sorrel *(roselle)*—A tropical plant grown for the bright red, fleshy sepals that surround the seed pod. The sepals are removed and used fresh or dried in beverages and jellies. They are available dried and packaged at health food stores; at West Indian food shops they can be found fresh or dried.

Soursop *(corossol, guanábana)*—A spiny, dark green heart-shaped fruit with cottony white flesh and a tart taste. It is used in beverages, ice creams, and sherbets. Outside of the Caribbean, it is somewhat difficult to locate fresh, but soursop nectar is available from Spanish *bodegas* by the name *guanábana.*

Sweet Potato *(batata)*—Having a reddish or pink skin and cream-colored flesh, this starchy root vegetable is baked or mashed. It is found in West Indian and Hispanic food stores.

Tamarind—A tree grown in the tropics. The brown, acidic pulp of the seed pod is used as an ingredient in condiments, candies, and beverages. The packaged pulp can be bought from West Indian stores; the nectar is widely available under the Spanish name, *tamarindo.*

Yams *(ñame, igname)*—Large edible roots, they vary in size, shape, and texture. Caribbean yams can be waxy, dry, or hard; they can be bland or sweet. Yams are cooked in soups and served as a side dish mashed, baked, or boiled. They should not be confused with Louisiana yam or sweet potato.

Index

About the Author

A native Jamaican, Dunstan A. Harris emigrated to the United States to pursue degrees in sociology and English at the University of Massachusetts. His career spanned teaching in California, researching for Time-Life Books in New York, and freelance writing and film-making, mostly on the subject of the Caribbean. For several years, Mr. Harris was involved in importing Caribbean foods to the United States. During that time he feasted, compared, and collected recipes from all over the Caribbean before settling down to write his own cookbook.